This is a helpful introduction to an important first century historian. It concentrates on how his writings relate to the New Testament, frequently confirming its history and illuminating its context.

Oliver Barclay,
Leicester

David Bentley-Taylor, a native of Hereford where he still lives in retirement, was involved as a young man in Christian service in China and Java before becoming travelling secretary of the International Fellowship of Evangelical Students from 1966 to 1974. He has written biographies of Henry Martyn and Augustine of Hippo. He has four sons, fourteen grandchildren and six great-grandchildren. He remarried after his first wife died in 1993.

JOSEPHUS
A Unique Witness

JOSEPHUS
A Unique
Witness

David Bentley-Taylor

Christian Focus

ISBN 1 85792 499 1

© David Bentley-Taylor

Published in 1999
by
Christian Focus Publications
Geanies House, Fearn,
Ross-shire, IV20 1TW, Great Britain

Cover design by Owen Daily

Contents

Epilogue: The Kingdom of Iron and the Kingdom of God 137

Preface

The Uniqueness of Josephus

Josephus was a first century Jew living in Jerusalem during most of the events recorded in the Acts of the Apostles. He was a younger contemporary of Paul. During his lifetime Luke, John, Peter, Paul and other Christians were writing the books and letters later brought together to form the New Testament. Josephus was not a Christian, but he knew about John the Baptist and he knew about Jesus, referring to them in his books with remarkable respect and observing that 'the tribe of Christians is with us to this day'. He was both a man of action and a very talented historian, describing in detail the terrible struggle between the Romans and the Jews in which he himself played so significant a role.

His great importance two thousand years later is due to the fact that the context of his career in Palestine was the same as that in which Jesus lived and the early Christian believers proclaimed their message. His magnificent descriptions of Jerusalem and of Galilee, with its lake and villages, are a delightful commentary on the Gospel narratives. His account of social and political conditions, of religious Jews and dominant Romans, confirms what the New Testament has to tell us. More than twenty of the prominent people mentioned in the first five books of the New Testament figure on a greater scale in the histories of Josephus, from Herod the Great to Felix and Festus, including such women as Herodias, Bernice and Drusilla. So his books are a unique companion to the New Testament, showing it to be a genuine product of that far away yet hugely influential era.

No other writer can compare with Josephus. He was right there, where Jesus had just been, on the lake and in the hills, at Cana and Capernaum, beside the Jordan, at the pool of Siloam and on the Mount of Olives. We can be thankful that he miraculously survived his adventurous youth and won through to a long retirement in Rome, which enabled him to record the destruction of Jerusalem and the Temple, along with much priceless data preserved by no one else.

My aim has been to make him accessible to those who might be put off by the length, complexity and frightfulness of his story. Those who have ears to hear what Jesus has to say will find it profitable, at quite a different level, to hear the words of Josephus too.

I have deliberately not raised technical questions, such as the significance of the Slavonic additions to the text of Josephus' works, and I have mostly avoided mentioning his estimate of the number of people involved on various occasions, which he may have been prone to exaggerate. But I by no means agree with those who maintain that his writings are so full of inventions and lies that we cannot know what really happened. My aim has been to make him accessible to those who might be put off by the length, complexity and frightfulness of his story. Anyone with ears to hear what Jesus has to say will find it profitable, at quite a different level, to hear the words of Josephus too.

Outline of main events

BC

73	Birth of Herod the Great
63	Pompey annexed Palestine to the Roman Empire
47	Julius Caesar made Antipater Governor of Judea
44	Assassination of Julius Caesar
40	Herod made King of the Jews
31	Suicide of Mark Antony and Cleopatra
25	Herod began to build Caesarea
19	Herod began to rebuild the Temple
5	Probable date of the birth of Jesus
4	Death of Herod at Jericho

AD

6	Archelaus replaced by Roman Governors
27-37	Pontius Pilate Governor of Judea
37	Birth of Josephus in Jerusalem
44	Death of King Herod Agrippa at Caesarea
52-59	Felix Governor of Judea
59-61	Festus Governor of Judea
60-61	Paul taken to Rome about this time
61	Death of James, brother of Jesus
66-70	War between Romans and Jews

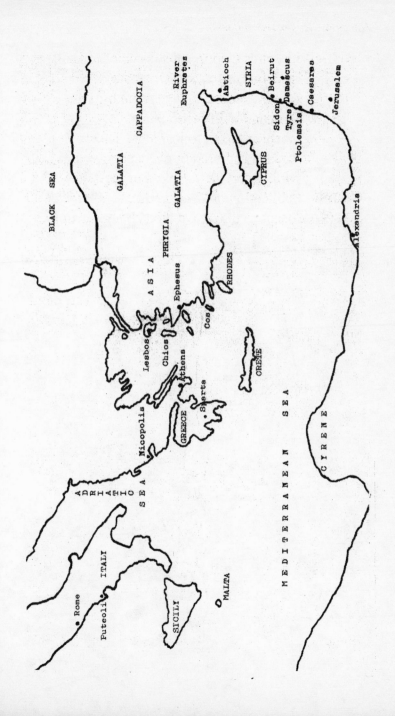

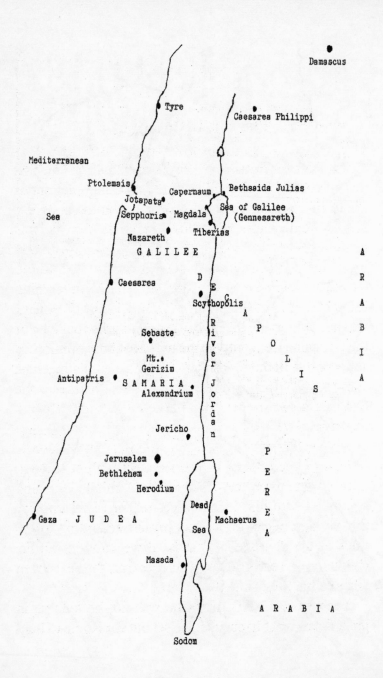

1

The Life of Josephus

'I was born in Jerusalem,' says Josephus, 'in the first year of Gaius Caesar', which was 37 AD, the year Pontius Pilate finished his time as Roman Governor in Judea. His father's name was Matthias. His family was distinguished, 'descended all along from the priests, and by my mother I am of royal blood.' It was not long before his remarkable memory and exceptional love of learning brought him to the attention of the authorities. 'When I was about fourteen the high priests and principal men of the city came frequently to me to find out my opinion on some points in the Jewish law.' At the age of sixteen he started investigating the views of the Pharisees, the Sadducees and the Essenes. 'When I was told about a man named Banus who lived in the desert, used no clothes except what grew on trees, ate no food except what grew of its own accord, and bathed frequently night and day in cold water to preserve his chastity, I imitated him and continued with him for three years. Then I returned to the city and began to conduct myself according to the rules of the Pharisees.' That is all we know about his childhood and early youth. He passes over the next seven years of his life in silence.

Then from 63 AD, when he was 26, he tells us in great detail what happened. He set out for Rome to help some priests he knew, 'very excellent people, who for some trifling reason had been imprisoned by Felix and sent to plead their cause before the Emperor.' He was impressed by hearing that 'they were not unmindful of piety towards God, even in their afflictions, but kept themselves alive with figs and nuts'. The Emperor at that time was Nero, and the Apostle Paul was already in Rome, as described in the last verses of the Acts of the Apostles.

'Our ship sank in the Adriatic Sea. There were about six hundred people on board. We swam for our lives all night. At dawn we sighted a ship of Cyrene and by God's providence eighty of us were rescued.' Like Paul, he was landed at Puteoli near Naples. In Italy he got to know a Jewish actor 'much beloved by Nero', through whom he met Poppea, Nero's wife. 'I took care, as soon as possible, to entreat her to get the priests released.' She not only succeeded in this but also gave him many presents before he returned home. So the trip was a great success. More important still, however, was the impression the visit gave him of the power of the Empire, the military skill and the sheer 'good fortune' of the Romans. The conviction that they were irresistible became fundamental to his thinking. Having grown up in the Jewish capital and then had a sight of the Gentile capital, he perceived it would be utter folly for the Jews to imagine they could stage a successful revolt against the Romans (*Life 3*).

No sooner had he returned to Judea, however, than he discovered that the ardent nationalists, bent on winning independence without delay by force, had won over large numbers of his contemporaries. He spoke out boldly in the hope of changing their minds. 'I laid before their eyes against whom they were proposing to fight and told them frankly that they were inferior to the Romans.' In the strongest terms he warned them that it would be madness to rebel: it could only lead to total disaster. 'But I was unable to persuade them.' There was at the moment no Roman Governor in office and the extremists had already got possession of the fortress of Antonia, the army headquarters alongside the Temple in Jerusalem. Listening to what Josephus said made many young men suspicious of him, 'as if I were of our enemy's party.' Suspecting he might get knifed, he took refuge first 'in the inner court of the Temple', then 'with the high priests and chief Pharisees', all of whom were very frightened and at a loss to know what to do. So acute was their danger that they had to pretend they agreed with the extremists. All they dared do was 'advise them to be quiet for the present'. Secretly they hoped the new Governor would come soon and bring strong enough forces to discourage an uprising, but when he did appear the nationalists scored a surprising victory, 'killing a great number of those that were with him.' In retrospect Josephus was to consider this 'a calamity for our whole nation', because it gave such encouragement to those who wanted war and believed they could win it. For about two years he had to live a double life, outwardly supporting the rebels but inwardly certain that their plans were suicidal (*Life 4-5*).

The Jewish leaders with whom he was friendly then decided to send him to Galilee, 'some part of which was still quiet', in the rather forlorn hope that he might be able to persuade 'the innovators' there to lay down their arms. He soon identified the towns which wanted to maintain their relationship to the Romans and those which favoured revolt. 'This I reported to the Sanhedrin in Jerusalem, asking what I should do about it.' In reply (*Life 70*) they entrusted him with the government of the province. Two priests had been sent with him, but they showed no administrative ability 'and were very ready to take bribes', so he dismissed them and they returned to Jerusalem.

Without naming them he refers in detail to 'two great men' who came to him from the rugged northern region of Trachonitis, 'bringing their horses, their weapons and their money'. They were evidently not Jews, for the Galileans wanted to force them to be circumcised if they intended to remain, but Josephus was instinctively attracted to them. 'I said that everyone ought to be free to worship God according to his own inclination. These men have come to us for protection and we should not cause them to regret it.' So he made sure they had all they needed, lodging them at Magdala by the lake. However, many people still felt that 'if they won't change their religion to the religion of those to whom they have fled for safety, they should not be allowed to live.' The rumour spread that they were probably wizards sent by the Romans to bring about the surrender of the country. 'I laughed at this allegation of witchcraft, pointing out that the Romans would not bother to maintain their huge army if they could overcome their enemies by employing wizards.' But in spite of all he could say, he realised the men might be attacked, so he bought their horses from them and took them across the lake by boat (*Life 23, 31*).

In such uncertain times he was always in danger himself, in spite of the numbers of men under his command. He fortified Tiberias, Magdala, Mount Tabor, and the naturally strong position of Jotapata to the north of Nazareth, laying up large supplies of corn in each, as he felt sure worse trouble lay ahead (*Life 37*). At times he may have spoken unwisely, for when two influential Jews were with him, 'I told them at supper time that I knew the power of the Romans was superior to all others, though I did not say so publicly' (*Life 35*). Many envied him because of the authority he had while still less than thirty years old. Living for a while 'in a Galilean village called Cana', he put a colleague named Silas in charge of the city of Tiberias. But then almost immediately Silas urged him to come if he did not want to lose the place: a rival had moved in with armed men on the pretext of needing to make use of the local hot baths. Taking two hundred soldiers Josephus travelled all night, arriving in the early morning to find a large crowd assembled in an open space. Climbing up onto some high point he began to address them, but a servant shouted to him that it was not a good moment for making a speech as his life was in danger. He leapt down at once and his men got him safely away in a boat. There were many such crises and miraculous escapes, 'due, I suppose, to God, who is never unacquainted with those who do as they ought to do.' Friends rallied to him, advising him to level Tiberias to the ground and make slaves of its inhabitants, 'but I did not comply with them, thinking it a terrible thing to begin a civil war' (*Life 16-19*). After that he made his base at Sepphoris, then the main town in Galilee, whose people had already decided not to resist the Romans. On that account they were alarmed at his arrival, so they got in touch with a robber chief named Jesus, offering him a handsome bribe to bring his large band of men and eliminate Josephus. Jesus craftily sent a message asking permission to come and pay his respects. Not knowing of the bribe, Josephus consented, but when the robbers were not far away one of them deserted and warned him. 'So I took armed men with me and went into the market-place, pretending I knew nothing of what was planned. I told the men manning the gate to admit only Jesus and one or two associates.' As soon as this was done and the gate shut, 'I ordered him to throw down his weapons. Seeing his small group surrounded, he was terrified and submitted. Then I called him to me on his own and told him I knew about his treachery and who had hired him. I assured him I would forgive him if he would repent and be faithful to me in future. On his promising to do so, I let him go and gave him leave to get his men together again' (*Life 22*).

Religious scruples entered into his problems too. One Friday 'I had already sent my men to their own homes because the next day was our Sabbath and I did not want the people of the town disturbed by a lot of soldiers. I myself could not take up arms on the Sabbath either, because our law forbids us to do so, however great our need.' Yet he knew there were plans to kill him, and his father in Jerusalem was pressing him to return. 'But I had a wonderful dream that very night. A certain person stood by me and said, "Put away all fear. You will not only get over these difficulties but many others too, and with great success; but remember that you have got to fight the Romans" ' (*Life 32, 42*).

Early one morning he was at the Place of Prayer in Tiberias, 'a large edifice, big enough to hold a lot of people'. It was proposed to hold a religious fast the next day, no weapons being brought, to show that 'with God assisting us, such weapons are useless'. Josephus felt sure this was a ruse to make it easy to murder him. 'But I was forced to comply, lest I should appear to despise a proposal that tended to piety. So I ordered two of my most faithful bodyguards to hide daggers under their clothes, while I myself wore my breastplate and girded on my sword in a way that concealed it.' Thanks to these precautions he again escaped unharmed (*Life 58*).

Picking out several important Galileans, 'I made them my friends and companions as I journeyed, and set them to judge cases brought before me. I got their consent in giving sentences myself, taking care to arrive at just decisions and to keep my hands clear of all bribery.' Such responsibilities rapidly developed his self-confidence and his ability to cope with whatever happened. For this one period in his life he could take action without having to obey anybody else. His aim was to avoid unnecessary bloodshed, 'preserve every woman from injuries', and keep Galilee in peace if possible (*Life 8-15*). He enjoyed it, but he was always in danger.

'Late one night, while I was feasting with my friends, a servant told me that a horseman had arrived and wanted to see me at once, so I had him called in. He did not greet me in any way, but just held out a letter and demanded an immediate answer to it. I asked him to sit down and have supper with us, but he refused, so I held the letter in my hand and talked about other matters with my guests.' His suspicions thoroughly aroused, Josephus glanced at the letter when no one was looking, then sealed it up again. 'Dismissing the others to their beds, I asked four of my intimate friends to stay with me and told my servant to get some wine ready. Still holding the letter in my hands, I ordered twenty drachma to be given to the man for the expenses of his journey. When he took the money and thanked me for it, I perceived that he loved money and could easily be caught out over it. So I invited him to drink with us, promising him a drachma for every glass of wine he had. He gladly embraced this proposal and drank a great deal in order to get more money. In the end he became so drunk that he could not keep the secrets with which he had been entrusted. I did not even need to question him directly to find out that there was treachery planned and I was doomed to die at the hands of those who had sent him' (*Life 44*).

Then in 66 AD, not much more than two years after

his return from Rome, all this rivalry and animosity among the Jews was dwarfed by the outbreak of the war of liberation against the Romans, to whom they had been subject for a hundred and thirty years (*Wars 2:22:1*). In spite of doubts about his loyalty, and his own grave reservations, 'at a mass meeting held in the Temple precincts to appoint additional generals', Josephus was made commander-in-chief of Jewish forces in Galilee (*Wars 2:20:3*). In the few months that remained before the Romans attacked, he personally supervised the strengthening of several fortified positions, particularly Jotapata, midway between the Lake of Galilee and the Mediterranean. 'I raised a large army of young men, equipping them with all the old weapons I could find. Knowing that the invincible might of Rome was chiefly due to unhesitating obedience and constant training, I reorganised our forces on the Roman model, appointing more junior commanders than before and putting the soldiers under decurions, centurions, and tribunes. Above all I urged them to imitate Roman discipline at every turn and to refrain from their besetting sins of theft, looting and defrauding their own countrymen, since men whose private lives are smirched have not only human enemies but God himself to contend with' (*Wars 2:20:5-7*).

Meanwhile, the Emperor Nero appointed Vespasian, a warrior of wide experience in Germany and England, to be the Roman commander. Titus, Vespasian's son, who was younger than Josephus, came with 'the world-famous 5th, 10th, and 15th legions', and there was soon 'an orgy of fire and bloodshed throughout Galilee'. Josephus managed to send a final letter to Jerusalem setting out his assessment of the hopeless situation. 'When raw levies are confronted by veteran troops, infantry by cavalry, undisciplined individuals by seasoned regulars, men with nondescript weapons by fully-armed legionaries, the issue can never be in doubt' (*Wars 3:2:2*).

From his bases on the coast, Caesarea and Ptolemais, Vespasian pressed inland with his army of infantry, cavalry, spearmen, bowmen, slingers, roadmakers and engineers, 'the Eagle at the head of every legion, the symbol of empire and the portent of victory' (*Wars 3:6:2*). At the sight of such a mighty cavalcade Jewish morale collapsed and Josephus' men 'fled in all directions'. Seeing 'nothing but disaster looming ahead', he rapidly took refuge with the best of his men at Jotapata, a naturally strong position, 'perched above a precipice, cut off on three sides by remarkably deep ravines, the only access being from the north, where the town was built on the lower slopes of the mountain.' The Romans levelled much of the ground, stripped the surrounding hills of their trees, collected huge piles of timber and stones, and began erecting towers. 'Vespasian set up his projector-throwers in a ring, 160 of them, to bombard the defenders on the wall.' In a synchronised barrage catapults shot lances into the air, stones of nearly a hundred-weight rained down, together with firebrands and dense showers of arrows, driving the Jews back from the wall. However, Josephus succeeded in building it higher and encouraged night sorties to set the towers on fire. There was plenty of corn in Jotapata but no spring, so water had to be strictly rationed as there was little rain in the summer, when the siege took place (*Wars 3:7:1-14*).

Not only was there intense fighting day and night, 'the siege-guns constantly in action', but Vespasian also brought up the ram, 'a huge weapon like the mast of a ship, fitted at the end with a great lump of iron in the shape of a ram's head. It was drawn back by a great number of men, who then with a gigantic united heave swung it forwards so that it struck the wall with the projecting iron. The first blows might be ineffective, but no wall was so thick and strong that it could stand up to such prolonged battering.'

The Jews defended themselves with amazing courage and resourcefulness, but were gradually worn down by incessant fighting, lack of sleep, and shortage of water. Constant bombardment with arrows, spears and heavy stones caused many casualties. In spite of all their efforts they could not prevent the ram from breaching the wall. Just before dawn on the forty-seventh night of the siege the Romans surged in, massacring everyone.

They were anxious to get hold of Josephus, but he, 'helped by some divine providence, jumped into a deep pit with a cave at the bottom, where he found forty important people and plenty of supplies.' At night he climbed up to see if escape was possible, but there were sentries all around. Then a prisoner was forced to betray him. Vespasian wanted to take him alive, so he offered him a safe conduct and tried to persuade him to come out. He was prepared to give in, but the other men were adamant, determined to commit mass suicide rather than surrender. Believing that 'self-murder is hateful in God's sight', he argued that only after a natural death will our immortal souls 'win the most holy place in heaven, from which when time's wheel has turned full circle they will be sent again to dwell in unsullied bodies'. But they crowded round him with swords in their hands, reviling him for his cowardice, each one apparently about to cut him down. In this desperate situation he called out to some of them by name, glared authoritatively at others, shook hands with many, or pleaded with them till he was ashamed of himself, turning to them again and again like an animal at bay. Even when there seemed no hope, they still respected him as their commander and no one could actually bring himself to strike him. In despair he yielded to them, proposing that they draw lots to kill one another in turn. Presumably it was Josephus who supervised or manipulated the process, for in the end only he and one other remained alive. The two of them agreed to surrender (*Wars 3:8:7*).

The exultant Roman soldiers dragged him before Vespasian, demanding that he be put to death at once, but Titus persuaded his father to spare him for the present and send him to Nero. Hearing this, Josephus boldly asked if he might speak to them privately. They agreed, so he told them, 'I come as the messenger of the greatness that awaits you. You will be Caesar, Vespasian, you will be emperor, you and your son here.' At first Vespasian assumed that Josephus was just lying to save his skin, but as time went on he gradually warmed to the idea. So, although he kept him in prison, he saw to it that he was well-treated and had enough to eat. (*Wars 3:8:9*).

It was the first week in July 67 AD and the war went on, but a year later came the news that Nero had met his end, which caused Vespasian to defer the final assault on Jerusalem as he waited anxiously to see who would come into power. Three Emperors rose and fell during 69 AD. Then in desperation the soldiers in Caesarea 'declared Vespasian emperor and called on him to save the Empire in such a dangerous crisis' (*Wars 4:10:4*). He was not inclined to accept, 'preferring the security of private life', but at that his officers and men crowded round him with drawn swords, threatening to kill him if he refused. Sensing the widespread demand for strong leadership and conscious of his own ability, Vespasian gave in and the campaign to sweep him to power in Rome rapidly gained strength. Needing to be sure of the loyalty of Egypt, the granary of the Empire, he and Titus spent some time at Alexandria. It was there that he set Josephus free, before sailing for Rome as soon as the winter was over. Titus took Josephus onto his staff and returned with him to Jerusalem. What then transpired, and the role Josephus played as the war reached its terrible climax, will be recounted in a later chapter.

After the destruction of the city in 70 AD Josephus accompanied Titus to Rome, where he remained for the rest of his life. Vespasian made him a Roman citizen, lodged him in what had formerly been his own house, giving him a pension 'and no small amount of land tax-free in Judea', so he adopted the Emperor's family name and became Flavius Josephus. He was only thirty-three years old, but his active life was over.

He made remarkably good use of his long retirement. First he composed in Aramaic a history of the whole war, 'having been an actor myself in many of its transactions and an eye-witness of most of the rest' (*Apion 1:10*). This he sent to the Jews living in Arabia and beyond the Euphrates in Parthia and Babylonia (*Wars: Preface 2*). Then he took immense trouble to master Greek and employed learned secretaries to assist him in translating his book into this language so universally used even in Rome itself. 'Nothing escaped my knowledge,' he insisted. 'During the siege of Jerusalem I saw and carefully wrote down what took place in the Roman camp and I knew all that deserters told us about conditions in the city, for I was the only one who understood their language. I was so confident that I had recorded the facts truthfully that I first presented the books to Vespasian and Titus, then to many Romans who had taken part in the war, as well as to Jews living in Rome' (*Apion 1:9*). Titus even 'affixed his own signature to my volumes and gave orders for their publication' (*Life 65*). In fact both Vespasian and Titus allowed him access to their 'memoirs', the records they had made at the time as the struggle proceeded (*Apion 1:10, Life 65*). And he had the help of King Agrippa, the man so prominent in Acts chapters 25 and 26, who had also found refuge in Rome and was able to inform

Josephus of many matters he would not otherwise have known (*Life 65*). Few historians in any age can have enjoyed such a rare combination of factors favourable for presenting a true account of great public events.

We should, however, acknowledge that Josephus was not free from some disadvantages and prejudices. It was impossible for a person in his situation to utter any word of criticism about the emperor on whom he was totally dependent. He wrote scathingly about previous Emperors and the wickedness of Roman governors such as Pontius Pilate, yet he could only report favourably on what Vespasian and Titus did. But the Jewish leaders could expect no mercy from him. He was totally opposed to the patriotic freedom fighters, the Zealots, who were prepared to sacrifice their lives in the conviction that God would support them in fighting for independence from Rome. From the beginning he had sensed that their policy of revolt was madness, which was bound to lead to the destruction of the country and the wholesale massacre of its people. He could only portray them as fools and villains who deserved the fate which overtook them. Moreover, loathed as he was by the patriots for having gone over to the enemy, Josephus was not unnaturally keen to justify his own behaviour in the fearful events in which he and his contemporaries were embroiled. None of these factors, however, diminish his significance for us. His narrative can only be broadly and thankfully accepted as a trustworthy account of momentous events in world history.

Whether we regard him as a traitor, a genius, or just a

very talented and intelligent young man caught up in the horrors and dilemmas of war, we can be grateful that he managed to survive the holocaust to tell us what happened to so many who had seen and heard Jesus in earlier days or listened more recently to the preaching of Paul. When Eusebius, the Bishop of Caesarea, started to write his 'Church History' almost three centuries later, he acknowledged his debt to him – 'taking the fifth book of Josephus' history in our hands, let us go through the tragedy of what happened.' To this day the terrible story he told proves that Christianity did not take root in an easier world than ours, but in an age when genocide and torture, cruelty and vice, racialism and injustice had come to a climax which, as Eusebius suggested, 'casts every other tragic drama into the shade.'

Although he had so much to say about his youth, we know almost nothing about Josephus' life in Rome. He had married in Alexandria before returning to Jerusalem with Titus. Three sons were born to him, but 'I divorced my wife, not being pleased with her behaviour. Afterwards I married a Jewess who had lived in Crete, whose parents were among the most illustrious in the country and her character beyond that of most women, as her future life demonstrated. By her I had two more sons' (*Life 1* and *76*).

He wrote two historical books. *The Wars of the Jews*, published in 75 AD, covers the last two centuries BC as well as the recent conflict. *The Antiquities of the Jews* starts with the creation of the world, retells the whole story of the Old Testament and Apocrypha, and ends with the outbreak of war with the Romans. It appeared eighteen years later, in 93 AD, to be followed by two much shorter books, his *Life* and *Against Apion*. The four together are not much shorter than the whole Bible.

It was at the close of his last book that he gave the fullest account of his religious convictions. 'God is the beginning, the middle and the end of all things,' he declared, 'the Governor of the universe. All men ought to follow Him and worship Him in the practice of virtue. Though known to us by His power, He is unknown to us in regard to His essence, but those who believe that God is inspector of their lives will not permit themselves to commit any sin.' He wrote enthusiastically about Moses, 'our legislator', by whose law we should live 'as under a father and a master', strictly avoiding drunkenness, adultery, abortion, homosexuality, and unnatural pleasures. He advocated 'the advancement of piety, being content with what you have, taking care of righteousness, a general love of mankind, and preferring a brave life of hard work to idleness and expensive living' (*Apion 2:15-42*).

The latest date mentioned by Josephus is 93 AD, when he was 56. We do not know how much longer he lived.

2

The Biography of Herod the Great

The New Testament begins with King Herod's massacre of the infants at Bethlehem, one of the last acts of his thirty-seven year reign. Only Josephus has preserved for us the full story of his life.

For over a century the Jews had been ruled by one of their own families, the Maccabees, but in 63 BC Pompey annexed their country to the Roman Empire. Before long the most prominent man in the region was an Edomite named Antipater, married to an Arabian, who proved so useful to the Romans that Julius Caesar made him a Roman citizen and appointed him Governor of Judea (*Wars 1:9:5* and *1:10:3*). Herod was one of his sons and in 47 BC he put him in charge of Galilee. At the age of 25, 'clothed in purple, with his hair finely trimmed and his armed men around him, Herod destroyed a band of robbers, so the grateful people sang songs about him in their villages' (*Antiquities 14:9:2*).

Pompey being dead, Mark Antony came to the eastern Mediterranean, only to fall in love with Cleopatra, the Egyptian Queen. Antipater was poisoned by a rival, which had the effect of enhancing Herod's importance when the Parthians suddenly crossed the Jordan and overran the whole country. He escaped to Alexandria. 'Cleopatra could not prevail upon him to stay in Egypt, because he wanted to get to Rome as quickly as possible', where he poured out his tale of woe to Antony.

The Parthians set up as their puppet king in Jerusalem a Maccabee named Antigonus, so Herod planned to ask Antony to support another Maccabee, a teenager named Aristobulus, whose sister Mariamne he was himself intending to marry. Antony discussed this with Octavian, the adopted son and heir of Julius Caesar, who was destined to become the Emperor Augustus. Remembering how useful Herod's father had been to Rome, they decided it would pay them to have another strong man on their eastern frontier. So they did something which had never occurred to Herod. They convened the Senate, introduced him to it, and Antony proposed making him King of the Jews. Everyone agreed, so when they came out of the senate-house, Herod stood between Antony and Octavian, the two most powerful men in the Empire, and 'Antony feasted him on the first day of his reign' (*Antiquities 14:14:1-5*).

On his return to Judea people flocked around him, 'some because of their friendship with his father, some because of his splendid appearance.' But Antigonus had a much better right to the throne, for Herod was just a private man, an Edomite too, 'only half a Jew'. Although Antony seconded two legions to help him, three years of confused fighting followed before Herod was able to besiege Jerusalem, 'pausing only to marry Mariamne in Samaria'. There was terrible slaughter when he stormed the capital and captured Antigonus. He bribed Antony to have him executed rather than taken to Rome to argue his case. And thus, as Josephus says, 'The government of the Maccabees ceased after 126 years and power came to Herod, a man of no eminent extraction' (*Antiquities 14:15:1-2* and *14 :14:16:4 : 15:1:1-2*).

Hyrcanus, Mariamne's grandfather, had been captured by the Parthians, and the Jewish population in Babylonia 'honoured him as their high priest and king'. Herod managed to persuade him to return 'so that they could share the royal authority', treating him with the greatest respect. Hyrcanus' daughter, correctly suspecting that Herod intended to do away with him, urged her father to write to the King of Arabia to ask his help in leaving Jerusalem. The bearer of the letter showed it to Herod, who told him to take it on and then bring back the reply to him. Armed with both letters, Herod convened the Sanhedrin and had Hyrcanus executed for plotting with a foreign power (*Antiquities 15:2:1-2* and *15:6:2*).

Meanwhile Mariamne wanted him to make her attractive brother Aristobulus the high priest. He decided to do so, but only because 'if once he had that dignity he could not leave the country'. The boy's mother, however, was so anxious about him that she wrote to Cleopatra, who urged her to bring him to Egypt without delay. They planned to escape by night in two coffins to a waiting ship. But again Herod was informed and caught them in the act. Professing forgiveness, he made up his mind 'to put this young man out of the way'.

'At the feast of tabernacles the boy, now 17, went up to the altar to offer sacrifices, wearing the ornaments of his high priesthood. He was extremely good-looking, taller than most men of his age, revealing in his whole bearing the noble family from which he came.' All the people regarded him with admiration and affection. When the festival was over, his mother entertained Herod at Jericho. In the evening he played around with Aristobulus in a childish manner, drawing him aside to a lonely spot. It was very hot, so a group of Herod's men decided to cool off in a large fish-pond beside the house. At first Herod and the young man watched the others bathing, but then, at Herod's suggestion, Aristobulus went in among them. 'As he was swimming they dipped him, plunging him under water as though in fun, keeping it up till he was drowned' (*Antiquities 15:3:3*).

'Every family in Jerusalem was overwhelmed with grief at the news.' Herod, weeping profusely, organised a magnificent funeral. But the boy's mother told the whole story to Cleopatra, who demanded that Antony punish the murderer, 'since it was he who had made Herod king of a country to which he had no right.' Antony ordered Herod to meet him near Antioch. He left his uncle Joseph in charge of the government, with orders to kill Mariamne if Antony killed him, for he feared Antony had already fallen in love with her. In spite of Cleopatra's strenuous efforts to persuade Antony to give Herod's kingdom to her, the presents Herod brought him and the talks they had over meals together soon convinced Antony that having given him great authority he ought to allow him to use it (*Antiquities 15:3:4-6, 8*).

On his return Herod had to cope with Mariamne. 'His love for her was not of a calm nature nor such as we usually meet with among husbands. His affection and his jealousy were so vehement that he asked her if Joseph had been too familiar with her. She denied it, saying all that an innocent woman could say in her own defence. Overcome with passion for his wife, he apologised, till they both burst into tears and embraced with tender affection.' But, just to be sure, he put Joseph to death 'without permitting him to come into his sight' (*Antiquities 15:3:8-9* and *7:7*).

Antony and Cleopatra then visited Judea together. Herod considered murdering her while he had the chance, but his advisers felt Antony would not tolerate it. In Josephus' opinion she was 'a wicked creature, the most prominent woman in the world at that time'.

Antony had given Cleopatra parts of Arabia and some districts in Judea near Caesarea and Jericho, but in 31 BC the two of them were defeated by Augustus at the naval Battle of Actium and compelled to commit suicide on their return to Alexandria. For the next forty-five years Augustus was sole master of the Empire.

Herod, however, had been Antony's man, so he was uncertain what Augustus would think of him. Placing Mariamne in one of the fortresses he had built with instructions for her to be killed if he failed to return, he sailed for Rhodes to meet the Emperor. On arrival he took off his diadem and boldly confessed how much he owed to Antony. He admitted sending him money and supplies. He even said he would have fought with him at Actium had he not been distracted by friction with the Arabians. 'After his defeat, I did not desert him,' he went on. 'I stayed with him, not as a soldier but as an advisor. I told him the only way to save himself was by killing Cleopatra and coming to an agreement with you. But he would not listen. And now, if you can leave him out of it and consider how I generally behave to those who benefit me, you will find me as true to you as I was to him.'

In reply Augustus restored his diadem and 'his crown was more firmly settled upon him than ever'. He welcomed the Emperor magnificently to Judea, riding beside him when the army moved on to Egypt and providing lavishly for the soldiers as they crossed the desert. On reaching Alexandria Augustus presented him with the four hundred Galatians who had been Cleopatra's guards (*Antiquities 15:6:5-7, Wars 1:20:1-3*).

When he told Mariamne all this good news she was sorry to hear it, for she knew what a danger he was to her. This made him furious, 'entangled between love and hatred'. His mother and his sister, both implacably hostile to Mariamne, augmented his hatred by telling him slanderous stories about her. Josephus felt that though she was a chaste woman, faithful to him, she had unwisely formed the habit of treating him saucily because she knew he was enslaved to her. 'One day about noon the King lay down on his bed to rest and called for Mariamne. She came in but would not lie down with him, showing contempt for him and bitterly reproaching him for killing her brother and her grand-father Hyrcanus.' To this he reacted violently, so his sister produced a story about a 'love-potion' Mariamne was supposed to have prepared for him. In irrational rage he tortured one of her eunuchs about this, then concocted an elaborate accusation and brought her to trial. Seeing how determined he was, the court pronounced sentence of death, so he had her executed. 'She went to her death with unshaken firmness of mind, revealing the nobility of her family even in the last moments of her life.' But Herod's rage soon gave way to devastating remorse and grief as passionate as his love had been for her while she lived, 'which looked like divine vengeance upon him for taking away her life' (*Antiquities 15:7:4-7*).

Equipped with limitless power 'and a murderous mind', Herod continued to put many people to death throughout his reign, including several of his own sons. But in spite of such wickedness, he was no idle despot. He showed extraordinary ability and enterprise in the construction of numerous magnificent buildings at home and abroad as well as by his skill in administrating his domain. It suited the Romans very well to have such a strong man in control on their eastern frontier opposite Parthia. He never wavered in loyalty to Augustus, to whom he dedicated 'a most beautiful temple of the whitest stone' near the source of the Jordan. Indeed Josephus recorded 'Augustus often said that the dominions of Herod were too small for the greatness of his soul, for he deserved to have the whole of Syria and Egypt as well' (*Antiquities 16:5:1*). He kept the Jews obedient to him, partly because of the merciless punishments which he inflicted on the slightest excuse, partly because he cared for them so well in times of distress. In 25 BC there was a prolonged drought, leading to famine, disease, and many deaths. Herod collected up the finest things in his palace and sent them to the Roman governor in Egypt in exchange for massive exports of corn, 'making sure everyone understood that this help was due to him.' So many sheep and goats died that there was a grave shortage of wool for making clothes, but he contrived to deal with that as well as mobilising workers at harvest time, 'so that no one in want was left destitute.' His success in coping with the crisis so impressed the Jews, 'and was so cried up among other nations' which also profited from his foresight, that for the time being people's feelings about him underwent a radical change. In the towns he made fine speeches, full of kind words, and he cultivated a good understanding with local community leaders, winning their friendship by handsome presents. So they tolerated his submissiveness to the Romans, which obliged him to break with the traditions of his own country (*Antiquities 15:9:5*).

He was served by three eunuchs, one to look after his drinks, one in charge of his supper, and a third who not only put him to bed but played a prominent part in government affairs (*Antiquities 16:8:1*). Josephus also says that one night he opened the tomb of King David and went into it, expecting to find money there. He had hoped to reach the bodies of David and Solomon, but got frightened when two of the men with him lost their lives (*Antiquities 6:7:1*).

For ten years a Roman named Marcus Agrippa was Augustus' general in Asia (*Antiquities 16:3:3*). Herod invited him to Jerusalem, 'assembling all the people in their festive clothes to receive him with acclamation', and they soon became close friends, as he entertained him regally in the fortresses he had built up and down the country for his own security. Augustus was so gratified that he added to Herod's kingdom regions north-east of the Sea of Galilee. What counted still more with Herod was that 'in Augustus' affections he was second only to Marcus Agrippa and in Marcus' second only to Augustus' (*Wars 1:20:4*). He visited Marcus in the Black Sea, sailing to Rhodes, Cos, Chios and Lesbos on the way and proving so useful to him in the management of his army and 'in giving him counsel in civic affairs' that when they parted 'Marcus embraced Herod in his arms'. He then returned via Cappadocia, 'great Phrygia' and Ephesus, conferring benefits on every city through which he passed (*Antiquities 16:2:1-4*).

* * * * *

Not for nothing is he known as Herod the Great. He was not merely an exceptionally wicked man, but also a genius who left his mark on the world. Josephus deplored the awful story of his crimes, but he recorded in similar detail his remarkable achievements such as the creation of the town of Caesarea, mentioned fifteen times in the Acts of the Apostles. 'He had noticed on the coast a place hitherto called Strato's Tower, which was in decay, but thanks to its admirable situation was capable of benefitting from his generosity. So he decided to rebuild it entirely with limestone, adorning it with a splendid palace. Nowhere did he show more clearly the liveliness

43

of his imagination. The whole of that shore had been harbourless, but by unshakeable determination he won the battle against nature and constructed a harbour larger than the Piraeus at Athens. The site was as awkward as could be, but he wrestled triumphantly with the difficulties. He lowered into twenty fathoms of water blocks of stone mostly fifty feet long, nine feet deep and ten feet broad. When the foundations had risen to water-level he built a mole 200 feet wide, half of it as a breakwater, the rest to support the encircling stone wall on which were spaced massive towers. There was a row of arched recesses where crews could land onto a ledge forming a broad walk. The streets of the town were laid out symmetrically. Opposite the harbour stood Caesar's beautiful temple, containing a colossal statue of him, an equally impressive one symbolic of Rome, a superb theatre, an amphitheatre, and the market place.' Under the streets Herod constructed a central sewage canal with numerous branches, so arranged that at high tide the sea penetrated the canals and washed them clean (*Antiquities 15:9:6-7* and *Wars 1:21:5-7*).

Starting in 25 BC it took Herod twelve years to set up this new city, which he named Caesarea in honour of Augustus. It became one of the largest places in the country with a predominantly Greek population, retaining its importance for over a thousand years.

* * * * *

The Antonia was a fortress in the heart of Jerusalem, 'towering over the Temple on its northern side', totally reconstructed by Herod. The name does not occur in the New Testament, but the barracks mentioned repeatedly in Acts chapters 21 to 23 were the Antonia, so called in honour of Mark Antony. 'It was built on a rock 75 feet high. The interior was like a palace but with wide courtyards where troops could encamp. There were towers at each corner, one of them 100 feet high, so that from it the whole Temple could be viewed. Where it joined the Temple colonnades, stairs led down and by these the guards descended, for a Roman infantry unit was always stationed there and at festivals was deployed along the colonnades fully armed, watching for any sign of popular discontent. The City was dominated by the Temple, the Temple by Antonia, so that Antonia housed the guards of all three' (*Wars 1:21:1* and *5:5:8*). This shows how the Romans were able to rescue Paul so quickly in Acts 21:30-40, Luke even mentioning the steps on which he stood to address the crowd.

* * * * *

Masada was the name given by the Maccabees to the gigantic isolated rock towering 1,700 feet above the west coast of the Dead Sea. The flat summit was three-quarters of a mile round. 'Herod enclosed it with an 18-foot wall on which he erected 37 towers, reserving the rich soil of the plateau for cultivation and large water-tanks. He constructed a magnificent palace and a fort just below the crest on the western side, where alone Masada could with great difficulty be climbed. It was thought he planned the fortress as a refuge in case the Jews tried to restore the Maccabees to power or Cleopatra persuaded Antony to give her Judea' (*Wars 7:8:3*).

* * * * *

In addition to these three immense undertakings, Herod carried out an extraordinary number of other substantial projects. 'There were deep ravines on every side of the fortress of Machaerus seven miles east of the Dead Sea, where John the Baptist was to be put to death. It commanded a fine view of Arab territory, so Herod decided to found a city there, enclosing a large area within walls and towers, inside which he constructed another wall round the actual summit, along with rain-water tanks and a palace of breath-taking size and beauty' (*Antiquities 18:5:1-2* and *Wars 7:6:1-2*).

The Herodium was his name for a hill a few miles south of Bethlehem which he turned into a stronghold by first increasing its height and then gouging a crater out of the summit. 'He encircled the top with towers and filled the crater with a superb palace, bringing in an unlimited supply of water at enormous cost and beautifying the approach with two hundred steps of white marble. He chose it as his burial place' (*Antiquities 15:9:4* and *Wars 1:21:10*).

He transformed Samaria by the fortress he built there and changed its name to Sebaste. Its walls were two miles long and he settled the place with 6,000 colonists, erecting in the centre a huge temple to Caesar Augustus (*Antiquities 15:8:5* and *Wars 1:21:2*).

'Choosing a site in the loveliest plain in his kingdom, where the soil was good, there were plenty of trees and a river, he founded the city of Antipatris, naming it after his father Antipater' (*Wars 1:21:9* and *Antiquities 16:5:2*). Paul was to spend a night there under guard (Acts 23:31).

Herod's enterprise and genius was not only to be seen in his own realm. 'At Antioch, the capital of Syria, he paved more than two miles of the main street with polished marble because of the mud, adding a colonnade from end to end to keep the rain off' (*Wars 1:21:11*). At Nicopolis in western Greece, the City of Victory built by Augustus to celebrate his triumph over Antony at nearby Actium, 'it was Herod who erected most of the public buildings' (*Antiquities 15:5:3*). Paul urged Titus to join him there one winter (Titus 3:12). 'Over and over again he gave money for construction in Rhodes and when the Temple of Apollo was burnt down he rebuilt it in such splendour that many people thought this the greatest of all his works' (*Antiquities 16:5:3* and *Wars 1:21:11*). Josephus felt he could go on for ever if he tried to list all the benefits Herod had conferred on others. At Sidon and Damascus he constructed theatres, at Beirut and Tyre temples and market-places. 'Even Athens and Sparta are full of Herod's offerings, are they not?' (*Wars 1:21:11*).

Yet one of his most remarkable achievements was

the revival of the Olympic Games, 'a gift not only to Greece but to every corner of the civilised world'. Seeing that they were declining for lack of funds 'and that the sole relic of ancient Greece was slipping away', Herod not only acted as President of one of the four-yearly meetings when on his way to Rome 'but endowed them for all time with an income big enough to make sure that his presidency would never be forgotten' (*Wars 1:21:11*).

Then he also inaugurated 'Caesar's Games' at Caesarea, gracing the first contest with valuable prizes, but Josephus strongly disapproved when 'he revolted against the laws of his country and corrupted the Jewish people by introducing such foreign practices at Jerusalem itself.' He built a large theatre with inscriptions glorifying the achievements of the Emperor, to which he added 'an amphitheatre in the plain'. Offering glittering prizes, he attracted the most outstanding performers in the Empire, 'calling men together out of every nation in honour of Caesar.' In addition to assembling any number of wrestlers, musicians and charioteers, he collected lions and other rarely seen animals, setting them to fight with each other or with condemned prisoners for the entertainment of the spectators. 'Foreigners were greatly surprised and delighted at the sheer size, character and danger of such displays', while Herod himself was no mean performer in horsemanship, archery and throwing the javelin. The huge crowds attracted by the Games were lavishly entertained with feasts and 'merrymaking at night on a scale no one had ever seen before' (*Antiquities 15:8:1, Wars 1:21:11*).

To crown all this, in 19 BC Herod set about rebuilding the Temple erected centuries before when the Jews returned from exile in Babylon. His aim was to increase its size, height, and grandeur so as to make it 'an everlasting memorial to himself.' He had to reassure the public that 'he would not pull down the existing building until everything was ready for rebuilding it, and he did not break his word' (*Antiquities 15:11:1-3, Wars 5:5:1-7*).

As was to be expected, he carried out his plan with remarkable thoroughness. 'He took away the old foundations and laid new ones. He also encompassed the entire Temple with large cloisters and a colossal outer wall, till it seemed no one else had so greatly adorned the Temple as he.' It took eight years to complete the enclosures, but the rebuilding of the actual Temple was done in only eighteen months, followed by tremendous celebrations, made all the more impressive because they were combined with 'the anniversary of the King's inauguration'. Improvements continued on a huge scale long after his death, so for decades Josephus watched what was being done. 'The magnificence of it all was remarkable, amazing to mind and eye.' When the work at last ceased in 64 AD eighteen thousand men lost their jobs (*Antiquities 20:9:7*).

This was Herod's Temple, the temple in which Jesus himself taught so often, where later on the disciples frequently gathered, and where Paul was almost lynched.

* * * * *

At the age of seventy Herod became seriously ill, so he made his will, bequeathing his kingdom to his son Antipas. 'As he despaired of recovering, he grew fiercer and was bitterly angry all the time.' It must have been in these days that he murdered the infants at Bethlehem.

He had recently erected a golden eagle over the main gate of the Temple. A band of students pulled it down and chopped it up with axes in broad daylight. He had them brought before him in the theatre at Jericho. As he could no longer stand up, he lay on a couch to harangue the people and then had them burnt alive. 'That very night there was an eclipse of the moon', generally presumed to be that of March 13, 4 BC (*Antiquities 17:6:4, Wars 1:33:2-4*).

He grew worse, constantly in pain – 'God's judgment upon him for his sins' – so he crossed the Jordan to seek relief from hot springs near the Dead Sea, then by being immersed in a bath of hot oil. Knowing how every one would rejoice at his death, 'he brought together the most eminent men of every village in the whole of Judea and had them locked up in the hippodrome' with instructions that they were to be killed as soon as he died, so that the whole nation would be plunged into mourning (*Wars 1:33:5-6*).

Five days before he died he had his son Antipater executed. Then he changed his will to make Archelaus his heir, Antipas tetrarch of Galilee and Perea, and Philip tetrarch of Trachonitis, the arrangement reflected in Luke 3:1. His sister Salome announced his death in the hippodrome and mercifully freed the prisoners (*Wars 1:33:7-8*).

So it was Archelaus who planned his sumptuous funeral. Thousands of soldiers, guards and servants walked in procession from Jericho to his burial at the Herodium above Bethlehem. His body was carried on a golden bier embroidered with precious stones and draped with purple. There was a sceptre in his right hand and a crown of gold on his head (*Wars 1:33:9*).

In spite of the contrast between his vices and his achievements, Josephus felt there was really no contradiction in his nature. His apparent virtues and his countless crimes flowed from one and the same polluted source. He was totally selfish. His one passion was to be honoured and praised. 'He had himself in view all the time' (*Antiquities 15:9:5* and *16:5:4*).

Death did not entirely remove his influence. Eight of his descendants are named in the opening five books of the New Testament.

Herod's Family

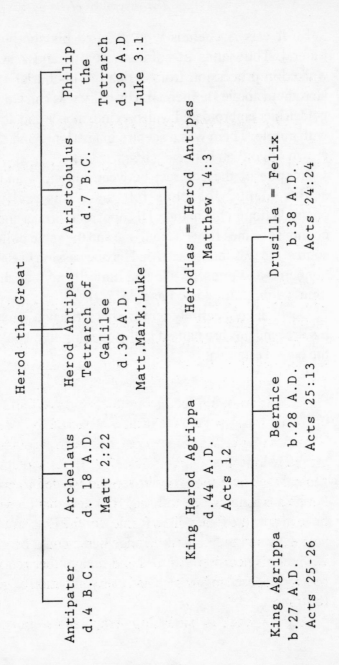

3

The Descendants of Herod the Great

Herod had nine wives, seven of whom bore him children (*Antiquities 17:1:3* and *Wars 1:28:4*). There were many sons, daughters, grandchildren and great-grandchildren. Only those mentioned in this book are shown in the chart opposite.

Archelaus

The first of Herod the Great's descendants to be mentioned in the New Testament is Archelaus. The news that he had succeeded his father so alarmed Joseph when he returned from Egypt with Mary and the child Jesus that he avoided him by going back to Galilee.

Archelaus and his younger brother Antipas (the Herod of the Gospels) were the children of Herod the Great's Samaritan wife, Malthace. They had been 'brought up privately in Rome' (*Antiquities 17:1:3*). As soon as the funeral was over the army in Jericho wanted to crown Archelaus king, but he refused. He knew that he would have to take the final will to Rome, for the Emperor was sole executor and no new arrangements could be made without his decision. Antipas and many other relatives bitterly opposed to him also had every intention of going to Rome.

After a week in mourning Archelaus went to the

Temple, sat dressed in white on a golden throne and delighted the crowds by promising to agree to all their demands about taxation and the release of prisoners. He explained to them that he would not assume royal power till Caesar had confirmed his succession. Passover time came on, but coincided with intense indignation about those who had been executed for cutting down the golden eagle. Such grave riots broke out that Archelaus sent in his troops, thousands of people lost their lives, and the festival had to be abandoned (*Antiquities 17:9:3*). He went on to Caesarea where he embarked for Rome, as did Antipas, their mother, and supporters of both sides, leaving Philip the tetrarch officially in charge under Varus, the Governor of Syria. As soon as they had gone civil war erupted on an even larger scale.

When they all got to Rome, Augustus was faced with the task of assessing the rival claims. 'Antipas and all the relatives who detested Archelaus' maintained that Herod's earlier will ought to take priority over the revision made when he was at death's door, 'his mind so decayed that he was incapable of logical thought.' They laid great emphasis on the recent slaughter at the Passover, 'the huge pile of corpses in the Temple', as evidence of what could be expected if Archelaus was in power. Archelaus, however, 'came forward and fell down at Caesar's knees without saying a word. The Emperor raised him up in the most gracious manner and declared that he deserved to succeed his father. But he made no definite announcement. He dismissed the company and thought over in private all he had been told' (*Wars 2:2:3-*

7). So there was a prolonged pause during which Malthace, mother of both claimants, died and letters came from Varus reporting disorder throughout the country, 'fire and bloodshed on every side', along with grave damage to the partially rebuilt Temple.

Augustus summoned a Council of leading Romans in the temple of Apollo which he had built within his palace. Also present on this historic occasion were fifty Jews allowed to come by Varus to plead for liberty to live under their own laws, who had the support of the eight thousand Jews living in Rome. Philip was sent too in the hope of securing a share in his father's estate if Augustus decided to divide it up. The Jews complained bitterly that 'they had endured more calamities at Herod's hands than their ancestors had done since the return from Babylon'. Insisting that 'Archelaus was the cruel son of that cruel tyrant', they begged Augustus 'to pity them, to unite their country with Syria, and to administer it through Roman officials'.

After giving a full hearing to both sides, the Emperor adjourned the meeting and a few days later announced his decision. He gave half Herod's kingdom, including Judea, Samaria and Jerusalem, to Archelaus with the title of Ethnarch (ruler of the people) and the promise that he would be made King if he proved worthy of it. The other half he divided between Antipas and Philip as Tetrarchs (rulers of a fourth part). To Antipas he allotted Galilee and Perea, to Philip the remoter areas east and north of the Sea of Galilee. He took the opportunity of separating from Judea the Greek city of Gaza and attaching it to

Syria. And he redistributed among many relatives the huge sum of money Herod had bequeathed to him. He acted cautiously in the hope of averting domestic strife.

All this we owe to Josephus, who passes over Archelaus' reign in silence beyond recording that he broke his promises and that his brutalities provoked both Jews and Samaritans to plead for his removal. It must have been at this time that Joseph decided to settle in the territory of Antipas rather than under Archelaus, whom Augustus recalled after only ten years and banished to Vienne in France. Perhaps the visit of Jesus to Jerusalem when he stayed behind in the Temple took place after Archelaus had gone. In his stead Augustus appointed the first of the Roman Governors, Coponius. The fifth such Governor was destined to be Pontius Pilate. So it was the failure of Archelaus and the thoughtful decisions of Augustus which brought about the political situation under which Jesus was later to teach and suffer (*Antiquities 17:11:1-4, Wars 2:6:1-3*).

Herod Antipas and Herodias

Herod Antipas was the Herod of the Gospels, the younger son of Malthace, the Samaritan wife of Herod the Great, and the brother of Archelaus, with whom he had been brought up in Rome. He is mentioned more than thirty times in the New Testament, where he is called just 'Herod' or 'Herod the tetrarch', once only 'King Herod'. The late change in his father's will, confirmed by the Emperor, left him in charge of Galilee and Perea, but he proved more successful than his brother, retaining power for forty years. Jesus alluded to him as 'that fox' (Luke 13:32), but Herod was very pleased when Pontius Pilate sent Jesus to him, having learned that he was from Galilee. He had for some time wanted to meet him and see him do a miracle, so he plied him with many questions. 'But Jesus gave him no answer' (Luke 23:9).

Tiberius, who succeeded Augustus as Emperor in 14 AD, viewed Herod Antipas with great favour, 'so he built a city in the best part of Galilee, at the Lake of Gennesareth, and called it Tiberias, compelling many people to move there and building them very good houses at his own expense' (*Antiquities 18:2:3*). It is mentioned only once in the Gospels, though the Lake is twice called the Sea of Tiberias.

Herod Antipas' wife was the daughter of the Arabian King Aretas (2 Corinthians 11:32), but on a visit to Rome he fell in love with Herodias, the wife of his half-brother Herod Philip (not the same as Philip the tetrarch), so he divorced her. In indignation Aretas invaded Galilee and got the better of Antipas' army. Josephus records that 'Some of the Jews thought the destruction of Herod Antipas' army came from God as a punishment for killing John the Baptist, a good man, who commanded the people to practise virtue towards one another and piety towards God, and so come to baptism. Antipas was afraid that the great influence John had over the population might incline him to raise a rebellion, for they seemed ready to do anything he advised. So he thought it best to prevent any mischief he might cause by putting him to death. Accordingly he imprisoned John at Machaerus and had him killed there' (*Antiquities 18:5:1-2*).

Shortly before he died in 37 AD Tiberius ordered Vitellius, the Governor of Syria, to form a league of friendship with the King of Parthia. A meeting was arranged to take place on the Euphrates, which formed the border between the two empires, and Herod Antipas went along too. 'A bridge was laid over the river. Each man came with his guards around him and they met in the middle of the bridge.' When the terms of peace had been fixed, 'Herod erected a sumptuous tent there and made them a feast' (*Antiquities 18:4:3-5*).

In time, however, Herodias became dissatisfied because, although her husband had been tetrarch for so long, the Romans had never recognised him as king. Another member of their huge family had gone to Rome where the new emperor, Gaius Caligula, made him king over what had been the tetrarchy of Philip. Envious of this, she felt her lazy husband should do the same. In the end her will prevailed and they went together. But Gaius' mind had already been poisoned against them: instead of making Antipas king he took his tetrarchy away from him and exiled both of them to France and Spain, where they died (*Antiquities 18:7:1-2, Wars 2:9:6*).

Philip the Tetrarch

This Philip, another son of Herod the Great, is mentioned in Luke 3:1 as tetrarch of several regions north-east of the Lake of Galilee, none of which are referred to again in the Gospels. All we know about him is derived from Josephus. 'His mother was Cleopatra of Jerusalem and he was brought up at Rome' (*Antiquities 17:1:3*). When Tiberius succeeded Augustus as Emperor in 14 AD 'Philip founded the city of Caesarea Philippi near the source of the Jordan', naming it after Tiberius and himself (*Wars 2:9:1*). It was the most northerly place reached in the ministry of Jesus, near which Peter made his famous confession, 'You are the Christ, the Son of the living God.' Philip also enlarged the village of Bethsaida, mentioned seven times in the Gospels, 'advancing it to the dignity of a city and naming it Julias after the daughter of Augustus' (*Antiquities 18:2:1*). And 'he married Salome, the daughter of Herodias' (*Antiquities 18:5:4*), who may have been the girl whose dancing led to the death of John the Baptist; they had no children. Josephus spoke rather well of Philip. 'He showed himself a person of moderation and quietness in the conduct of his life and government. He constantly lived in the region that was subject to him. He used to make his progress through it with a few chosen friends. When anyone met him who wanted his help, he made no delay but sat down wherever he happened to be and heard his complaint. When he died at Julias he was carried to the monument which he had already erected for himself and buried with great pomp' (*Antiquities 18:4:6*). This took place in the twentieth year of the reign of Tiberius, in 34 AD, shortly after the crucifixion of Christ, by which time he had ruled for 37 years (*Antiquities 18:4:6*).

Herod Agrippa

The whole of the twelfth chapter of the Acts of the Apostles is concerned with this 'King Herod', always called 'Agrippa' by Josephus, who told his story in great detail. He was one of the many grandchildren of Herod the Great, who had put his father Aristobulus to death. Acts 12 tells how he killed the Apostle James, arrested Peter, and then died suddenly himself.

In youth he lived in Rome so extravagantly that he ran out of money, returned to Judea, was tempted to commit suicide, and was financially rescued by Herodias, his sister. For a while he stayed in Tiberias, then returned to Italy and contrived to visit the Emperor Tiberius on Capri Island. He became a close friend of Gaius Caligula, who was destined to succeed Tiberius. Once when they were sitting in a chariot together he expressed the hope that Tiberius would not last much longer. Their driver overheard this remark, so Herod Agrippa found himself in prison for six months, till Tiberius died in 37AD. Gaius at once 'sent for Agrippa, had him shaved, made him change his clothes, put a diadem on his head, and appointed him King of the Tetrarchy of Philip, who had recently died' (*Antiquities 18:6:10*).

Herod Agrippa's influence then had a lot to do with the banishment of Herod Antipas and Herodias by Gaius, who added their tetrarchy to his. And when Gaius was assassinated in 41 AD Herod Agrippa was so useful to Claudius in obtaining the succession that he was rewarded by being given the entire kingdom formerly ruled by his grandfather. Josephus even calls him

'Agrippa the Great' (*Antiquities 18:5:4*).

His power lasted only seven years. 'He was a great builder, particularly in Beirut, where at enormous cost he erected a theatre and an amphitheatre, bringing in all kinds of musicians who made the most delightful music and setting hundreds of gladiators to fight each other as a form of recreation in peacetime.' Josephus, however, thought him an improvement on Herod Antipas, 'a mild man, humane to foreigners, gentle and compassionate, very liberal in his gifts. He loved to live constantly in Jerusalem and was careful to observe the laws of his country' (*Antiquities 19:7:34*).

In 44 AD he went to Caesarea to celebrate a festival in honour of Claudius. Josephus' account of what happened is an extraordinary parallel to Acts 12:19-24. 'On the second day of the festival he wore a garment made of silver and came into the theatre early in the morning. The sun's rays illuminated the silver in an astonishing way, so the people cried out that he was a god. He did not rebuke them or reject their flattery, but a severe pain arose in his abdomen, increasing rapidly. He was carried into the palace and the rumour spread that he was going to die. The crowd sat in sackcloth with wives and children, beseeching God for his recovery. The King rested in a room high up, from which he could see them lying prostrate on the ground below. For five days he was worn out by the pain, then he died. He was 54 years old, having reigned four years under Gaius and three years under Claudius' (*Antiquities 19:8:2*).

This gives us the certain date of 44 AD for the twelfth

chapter of the Acts of the Apostles. Most helpfully Josephus recorded the ages of his children when he died: his son Agrippa was seventeen, Bernice sixteen, and Drusilla six (*Antiquities 19:9:1*).

Agrippa and Bernice

Agrippa and Bernice were brother and sister, the great-grandchildren of Herod the Great, the children of Herod Agrippa of Acts 12. Agrippa had been in Rome when his father died at Caesarea, but the Emperor Claudius felt he was too young at seventeen to succeed to the throne, so he brought the kingdom under direct rule, sending Cuspius Fadus as Governor (*Antiquities 19:9:2*). Five years later, in 49 AD, he started to give parts of the country to Agrippa (*Antiquities 20:5:2, 20:7:1, Wars 2:13:2*), though his power was largely nominal. In particular, the care of the Temple was committed to him (*Antiquities 20:9:7*). Nero succeeded Claudius in 54 AD, so in his honour Agrippa enlarged Caesarea Philippi, changing its name for a while to Neronias, for such authority as he had was mainly north of Galilee. He devoted much time and money to Beirut, where he built a theatre and 'adorned the entire city with statues, indeed transferring to it almost all that was ornamental in his kingdom, which made him exceptionally unpopular at home' (*Antiquities 20:9:4*).

More trouble with his subjects arose when Festus became Governor in 59 AD. 'King Agrippa built himself a very large dining-room in his palace in Jerusalem. It commanded a splendid view over the city. He could lie down there and eat there, observing all that was done in the Temple down below. The Jews were highly displeased, specially because he could see the sacrifices being offered, so they built a wall to block his view. His indignation at this was fully shared by Festus, who ordered the Jews to demolish it. They besought him to allow them to send ten men to Nero about the matter, and he agreed. When Nero heard what they had to say, he not only forgave them for what they had done but also allowed the wall to stand. He did this to please his wife Poppea, who was a religious woman and had specially requested this favour from him' (*Antiquities 20:8:11*).

Since Festus died in 61 AD, it was almost certainly in 59 AD that Agrippa and Bernice visited him at Caesarea while Paul was his prisoner, as described so graphically in chapters 25 and 26 of the Acts of the Apostles, in which four of Agrippa's remarks are preserved:

Acts 25:22: 'Agrippa said to Festus, "I would like to hear this man myself."'

Acts 26:1: 'Agrippa said to Paul, "You have permission to speak for yourself."'

Acts 26:28: 'Agrippa said to Paul, "Do you think that in such a short time you can make me a Christian?"'

Acts 26:32: 'Agrippa said to Festus, "This man could have been set at liberty if he had not appealed to Caesar."'

When the war with Rome began in 66 AD Agrippa chanced to be in Egypt. The Jews burnt down his palace in Jerusalem. Bernice had stayed in the capital 'to perform a vow to God'. Twice widowed before she was

21, she tried to disprove the charge that she was living with her brother by persuading the King of Cilicia to be circumcised and marry her. Then, 'abandoning both him and the Jewish religion', she went back to her brother (*Antiquities 18:5:4, 20:7:3, 19:5:1*).

When Agrippa reached Jerusalem the people besought him to deliver them from Gessius Florus, but he was powerless to do anything of the sort. With Bernice beside him, he struggled to persuade them that it was futile to resist the Romans. Josephus, who precisely shared his views, reports him as arguing that the Greeks, the Macedonians, the French, the Spaniards, and 'even the Germans with their inexhaustible manpower' had submitted. 'Consider the defences of the Britons. They are surrounded by the ocean, yet the Romans crossed the sea and enslaved them. Will you alone refuse to serve the masters of the whole world?' At that the people started to stone him and he had to 'retire to his own kingdom in the north'. In the struggle for independence he had decisively sided with the imperialists. When Vespasian arrived at Antioch to take control of the campaign against the patriots, 'he found Agrippa awaiting him with the whole of his army' (*Wars 3:2:4*). After overrunning Galilee and capturing Josephus, Vespasian 'decided to acquaint himself with Agrippa's kingdom', so he marched his army to Caesarea Philippi and rested his troops for three weeks (*Wars 3:9:7*).

Just as Vespasian was about to move against Jerusalem, news came that Nero was dead and had been succeeded by Galba, so Vespasian sent his son Titus to pay homage to the new emperor and 'to seek instructions for settling the Jewish problem'. Agrippa and Bernice 'embarked for Rome along with him', but when they reached Greece they heard that Galba had been killed. Titus at once returned to his father in Caesarea, but 'Agrippa decided to complete his journey as if nothing had happened' (*Wars 4:9:2*).

Like Josephus, Agrippa spent the rest of his life in Rome. In his biography Josephus speaks of receiving sixty-two letters from the King, who warmly commended his book, *The Wars of the Jews*. But he also records that by 93 AD Agrippa had died (*Life 65*). He and Bernice were the last descendants of Herod the Great to leave their mark on history.

Dates of the twelve Roman Emperors and twelve Roman Governors of Palestine mentioned by Josephus

The Roman Emperors

Julius Caesar	49 - 44 BC
Augustus (Octavian)	44 BC - 14 AD
Tiberius	14 - 37
Gaius (Caligula)	37 - 41
Claudius	41 - 54
Nero	54 - 68
Galba	
Otho	69
Vitellius	
Vespasian	70 - 79
Titus	79 - 81
Domitian	81 - 96

The Roman Governors

Coponius	6 - 9 AD
Marcus Ambivius	10 - 13
Annius Rufus	13 - 15
Valerius Gratus	16 - 27
Pontius Pilate	27 - 37
Cuspius Fadus	44 - 45
Tiberius Alexander	46 - 48
Ventidius Cumanus	49 - 51
Felix	52 - 59
Porcius Festus	60 - 62
Albinus	62 - 64
Gessius Florus	64 - 66

4

The Romans – Emperors, Governors and Army

Emperors

1. *Julius Caesar*. Assassinated 44 BC
He is not mentioned in the New Testament, though the title 'Caesar', which originated with him, occurs frequently. Josephus reckons him to be the first Emperor (*Apion 2:5*). Thanks to Josephus we know that it was his friendship with Herod the Great's father Antipater which greatly contributed to the latter's rise to power and thus to Herod's (*Antiquities 14:8:1-5, Wars 1:9:3 to 1:10:4*).

2. *Augustus*. 44 BC to 14 AD
Luke 2:1: 'In those days Caesar Augustus issued a decree that a census should be taken of the entire Roman world.'

This is the only allusion to Augustus in the New Testament, though in the Authorised Version the name also occurs at Acts 25:21, 25 and 27:1 as a translation of the Greek word *sebastos*, meaning 'his Majesty', that is 'the Emperor'. Augustus is really the title conferred on Julius Caesar's adopted son and heir in 27 BC and then borne by subsequent Emperors too.

Josephus constantly refers to him in his biography of Herod the Great and in recounting the rise and fall of Archelaus. He died some years after the visit of the child

Jesus to the temple in Jerusalem. Josephus reckons he ruled for 57½ years, 'fourteen of them together with Mark Antony' (*Antiquities 18:2:2*).

3. *Tiberius*. 14 to 37 AD

Luke 3:1: 'In the fifteenth year of Tiberius Caesar. . .the word of God came to John.'

This is the only direct allusion to Tiberius in the New Testament, but it fixes the beginning of the ministry of John at 29 AD. The town of Tiberias was called after him and the Lake of Galilee described as 'the Sea of Tiberias' (John 6:1; 21:1). He was Emperor throughout the public life of Jesus. So 'Render to Caesar the things that are Caesar's' refers to him, as did the words of John 19:12-15, 'If you let this man go, you are no friend of Caesar. Anyone who claims to be a king opposes Caesar.. . .We have no king but Caesar.'

Josephus points out that 'it was Tiberius who sent Pilate to be governor in Judea' (*Wars 2:9:2*), though he blames the Emperor for being 'a delayer of affairs' since the two governors he appointed each had to stay for ten years before being replaced. He often mentions Tiberius' long residence on Capri Island, where Herod Agrippa (the Herod of Acts 12) visited him and was for a time well received before 'being kept in rigorous confinement for six months' till Tiberius died (*Antiquities 18:6:4, Wars 2:9:5*). 'He was more given to astrology and divination than any other Roman Emperor. He was fierce by nature, easily inflamed by irrational hatred, making death the penalty for the slightest offense, so that he brought great misery on the best Roman families' (*Antiquities 18:6:5, 8, 10*).

Josephus reckoned him the third emperor (*Antiquities 18:2:2*). He died the year Josephus was born, about the time of the conversion of the Apostle Paul (Acts 9).

4. *Gaius Caligula*. 37-41 AD

He is not mentioned in the New Testament, but Josephus records in detail how he banished Herod Antipas (the Herod of the Gospels), brought Herod Agrippa (the Herod of Acts 12) to such power, and attempted to erect a statue of himself in the Temple.

5. *Claudius*. 41-54 AD

Acts 11:28: 'This happened during the reign of Claudius.'

Acts 18:2: 'Claudius had ordered all the Jews to leave Rome.'

Early in his reign Claudius initiated the conquest of Britain. He is the only person named in the New Testament whom we know to have come to England. His accession and the invasion must have taken place about the time when 'the disciples were called Christians first at Antioch' (Acts 11:26).

Josephus says that 'while Claudius was a private person he applied himself to learning, specially Greek learning', and 'never meddled with public affairs' (*Antiquities 19:3:1-2*). He was alarmed when the murder of Gaius suddenly made it possible that he would be emperor. However, 'he was encouraged, partly by the soldiers, partly by the persuasion of King Herod (the

Herod of Acts 12), who exhorted him not to let such an opportunity slip out of his hands' (*Antiquities 19:4:1*).

6. *Nero*. 54-68 AD
Acts 25:8-12: 'I appeal to Caesar' (Acts 25:21, 25, 26; 26:32).

Acts 28:19: 'I was compelled to appeal to Caesar.'

Nero's name does not occur in the New Testament, but he was the Emperor to whom Paul appealed and during whose reign he lived for two years in Rome (Acts 28:30). There may be another allusion to him in 2 Timothy 4:16-17: 'At my first defense no one came to my support. . .but the Lord stood at my side. . .and I was delivered from the lion's mouth.'

Josephus mentions Nero's 'abuse of power and how he committed the management of affairs to vile wretches', and put to death his mother, his wife and many other illustrious persons whom he accused of plotting against him (*Antiquities 20:8:2*). On his own early visit to Rome he did not meet Nero.

7. *The Emperors after Nero*
In the memorable words of Suetonius, another first century historian, 'With Nero the line of the Caesars became extinct and the Empire drifted uneasily through a year of revolution in which three successive Emperors – Galba, Otho, and Vitellius – lost their lives through violence.'

Into the breach stepped a new imperial line, the Flavian family, in the person of Vespasian (70-79) who was to be succeeded by his sons, Titus (79-81) and Domitian (81-96). Of them Josephus had much to say, but no sure link can be established between the New Testament and these Emperors, for its historical context is the period from Augustus to Nero. Yet it is remarkable that Josephus describes how the Flavian dynasty originated at Caesarea when 'the soldiers declared Vespasian emperor'. Suetonius, moreover, says Vespasian was encouraged to accept by the words which had been spoken to him by 'a distinguished Jewish prisoner named Josephus' (*The Twelve Caesars 7:1, 10:1,* and *10:5*).

The Roman Governors

As long as Herod the Great was alive, there was no need for a Roman governor in Judea. Augustus hoped Archelaus would replace his father satisfactorily, but after ten years banished him and sent Conponius 'to have the supreme power over the Jews, including the right to inflict capital punishment'. During the next thirty years five men held this difficult post, the fifth being Pontius Pilate, who ruled from 27 to 37 AD. Josephus passes very briefly over the first four but then relates several incidents involving Pilate which vividly endorse the impression of him given by the Gospels, where he is named more than fifty times (*Antiquities 18:2:2*).

Pontius Pilate

The Governor always resided at Caesarea, 'but Pilate sent his army up to Jerusalem to take their winter-quarters there in order to abolish the Jewish laws.' He ordered the soldiers to take with them banners on which the Emperor was depicted, sending them in at dead of night because he knew the Jews would not approve. The previous governors had deliberately avoided doing this. When they saw what had happened, crowds of people went down to Caesarea to beseech him to remove the offending banners, but he refused to dishonour the Emperor by consenting to them. However, they stayed on, trying to persuade him. By the sixth day his patience had run out. Mustering soldiers with weapons ready, he 'sat on his judgment seat' and then suddenly commanded them to surround the mob. He announced he would have them killed unless they ceased to disturb him and went home. To his astonishment they all threw themselves on the ground and bared their necks, saying 'they would rather die than have the wisdom of their laws transgressed'. This so deeply moved him that he yielded and had the banners brought back to Caesarea (*Antiquities 18:3:1*).

But then Pilate 'stirred up further trouble by using the sacred money known as Corban' to construct a fifty-mile-long aqueduct to improve Jerusalem's water supply. This so infuriated the populace that when Pilate visited the capital they surrounded his tribunal in thousands and shouted him down. Anticipating something like this, he sent his men into action and many lives were lost. It is possible that this was the incident referred to in Luke 13:1 when people 'told Jesus about the Galileans whose blood Pilate had mixed with their sacrifices' (*Antiquities 18:3:2*).

'Now there was about this time Jesus, a wise man.' Josephus goes on, 'if it be lawful to call him a man, for he was a doer of wonderful works, a teacher of such men as receive the truth with pleasure. He drew over to him both many of the Jews and many of the Gentiles. This man was Christ. And when Pilate, at the suggestion of the principal men among us, had condemned him to the cross, those that loved him at the first did not forsake him, for he appeared to them alive the third day, as the divine prophets had foretold these and ten thousand other wonderful things concerning him. And the tribe of Christians, so named after him, are not extinct at this day' (*Antiquities 18:3:3*).

This famous passage of only ninety-one Greek words – shorter than the first six verses of Mark's Gospel – is the earliest known description of Jesus outside the New Testament. It is a remarkably comprehensive statement, alluding to his wisdom, his deeds, the truth of his teaching, his crucifixion, his resurrection, and the numerous Old Testament prophecies he fulfilled, hinting at his possible deity and identifying him as the Messiah. It attributes his condemnation primarily to leading Jews, but also to Pilate.

Some have thought a Christian must have inserted this paragraph into Josephus' manuscript, or touched up what he wrote, but this is guesswork and cannot be proved. It is also unnecessary, for Paul's substantial Epistle to the Romans, written many years earlier, shows that there had long been considerable numbers of Christians in Rome, so some knowledge of what they believed must have become widespread. Having spoken cordially of John the Baptist, it would have been strange if Josephus had not mentioned his far more influential successor.

He then goes on to report how Pilate clashed with the Samaritans. An imposter gathered them at Mount Gerizim, professing to show them where Moses had buried some sacred vessels. Pilate sent in his troops, who killed as many of the crowd as they could. He then put the leaders to death, but the Samaritan senate appealed to Vitellius, at that time Governor of Syria, accusing Pilate of murder, since the Samaritans had had no intention of revolting against the Romans. Vitellius sent him to Rome to answer the charge before the emperor, but Tiberius had died before Pilate got there and it is not known what happened to him (*Antiquities 18:4:1-2*).

After the removal of Pilate and the death of Tiberius in 37 AD, Herod Agrippa (the Herod of Acts 12) was so favoured by his successors, Gaius Caligula and Claudius, that for seven years no new governor was appointed. But the power of Agrippa terminated suddenly at Caesarea in 44 AD. Since Claudius felt his son was too young to succeed him, the line of governors was resumed (*Wars 2:11:6*). Josephus criticises later governors severely but speaks favourably of the first two, Cuspius Fadus (44-45) and Tiberius Alexander (46-48), 'who by abstaining from all interference with the customs of the country kept the nation at peace'. This must have been during the first of Paul's missionary journeys and the council of Christian leaders held in Jerusalem, as described in Acts 13–15.

Josephus has a lot to say about Tiberius Alexander, an Alexandrian Jew whose conversion to the Roman cause was even more radical than his own. His father, 'a person outstanding among all his contemporaries and eminent for his piety', was the leader of the large Jewish community in Alexandria, yet his son not only 'did not continue in the religion of his family', but emphasised his change of loyalties by adopting the name of the Emperor (*Antiquities 20:5:2*). Such were his abilities that later on he was to rise to the highest civil and military posts. Nero was to 'entrust him with the government of Egypt' (*Wars 2:5:1*). In that capacity he gave invaluable support to Vespasian before he went to take the empty throne in Rome (*Wars 4:10:6*). At a crucial moment in the siege of Jerusalem, as the chief of Titus' general staff, he was called into conference with the five commanders of the most famous legions (*Wars 6:4:3*). In due course he came to be related by marriage to King Agrippa and Bernice (*Antiquities 20:7:3*). And it was while he was Governor in Judea that 'a great famine happened there' (*Antiquities 20:5:2*), presumably the one said to have occurred during the reign of Claudius in Acts 11:28. Josephus represents him as doing his best 'to recall the Jews to reason without recourse to arms, entreating them not to provoke the Roman soldiers to take action' (*Wars 2:18:7*).

He was succeeded by Cumanus (49-51) who pleased the Jews when he executed a man who had torn in pieces a copy of the Mosaic law, but then supported the Samaritans in a bitter conflict over the murder of a

Galilean on his way to Jerusalem. He accompanied representatives of both sides to Rome, but Herod Agrippa was there too so Claudius was induced to favour the Jews, banish Cumanus, and send Felix to Palestine in his stead (*Wars 2:12:1-7*).

Felix

Felix owed his appointment over Judea, Samaria and Galilee partly to his brother Pallas, who stood high in the imperial favour (*Wars 2:12:8*), and partly to the Jewish high priest Jonathan, who had specially asked Claudius to send him. He was to retain the post for seven years, for the last two of which, 57 to 59, Paul was to be his prisoner, as related in Acts 24 (*Antiquities 20:8:5*).

After taking up residence in Caesarea, he saw Drusilla, the great-grand-daughter of Herod the Great, 'and fell in love with her, for she exceeded all other women in beauty.' The ruler of Homs in Syria had submitted to circumcision in order to marry her, but Felix sent to her a Cypriot Jew 'who pretended to be a magician', promising through him that 'if she would not refuse him he would make her a happy woman'. She had been so badly treated by her older sister Bernice on account of her good looks that 'she was prevailed upon to transgress the laws of her forefathers and marry Felix', who was uncircumcised. She was still in her late teens (*Antiquities 19:9:1*). Together they listened to Paul talking to them about faith in Jesus Christ, righteousness, self-control, and judgment to come (Acts 24:24-26). The couple had a son who perished in his youth with his wife at Pompeii 'at the conflagration of the mountain Vesuvius in the days of Titus Caesar' (*Antiquities 20:7:1-2*) in 79.

Josephus gives Felix credit for tackling the deteriorating conditions in the country, crucifying robbers, and taking captive a brigand leader to whom he had given a safe conduct. Jonathan the high priest, feeling some responsibility for him, kept giving him advice on how to improve his administration. Felix was so irritated by this that he arranged his murder, allowing armed assassins into Jerusalem 'as if they were going to worship God'. This crime encouraged similar murders at public festivals, even in the Temple. Josephus came to feel it marked a turning point. 'This seems to me to have been the reason why God, out of His hatred for the wickedness of these men, rejected our city and no longer esteemed the Temple pure enough for Him to inhabit' (*Antiquities 20:8:5*).

Day-time murders became so common and criminals so regularly escaped detection that fear, 'worse than the calamity itself', gripped the citizens (*Wars 2:13:3*). A new phenomenon followed. 'Men who claimed divine inspiration deluded the people, inducing multitudes to follow them into the wilderness, pretending they would see signs and wonders performed by God's providence.' Felix sent soldiers to round up the crowds and many lives were lost. Then came an Egyptian alleging he was a prophet, who called everyone to the Mount of Olives, asserting that at his command the walls of Jerusalem would fall down. Felix took immediate action. Four hundred people were killed, but the Egyptian himself escaped (*Antiquities 20:8:6*). The incident is mentioned in Acts 21:38, when the commander of the Roman garrison suspected Paul might be the missing Egyptian.

In Felix' time serious trouble broke out in Caesarea, whose population was part Jewish and part Syrian. The Jews claimed preeminence because Herod had created the town, but the Syrians insisted that it had been a Greek city long before that, when not a single Jew was to be found there. The Jews were the wealthier community, but the Syrians had the support of the Roman troops, most of whom came from Syria. When they started throwing stones at each other, 'Felix saw that this quarrel had become a kind of war, so he came one day into the market-place, threatened the Jews, and allowed his soldiers to plunder some of their houses, which were full of riches.' Happily, when the more moderate Jews begged him to give the offenders time to repent, he agreed to do so (*Antiquities 20:8:7-8, Wars 2:13:7*).

The remarkable statement in Acts 24:22 that 'Felix was well acquainted with the Way' is a reminder that there had been Christians in Caesarea for some time (Acts 8:40; 21:8-16), even in the Roman garrison (Acts 10:27-48), and suggests he had had some contact with them. Although he had frequent talks with Paul, he left him in prison when he was replaced in 59 'because he wanted to grant a favour to the Jews' (Acts 24:27). They hated him and sent a deputation to Rome to accuse him. In Josephus' opinion Felix would have been punished had Nero not been influenced by Pallas (*Antiquities 20:8:9*).

Porcius Festus

Porcius Festus, sent by Nero to succeed Felix as Governor in 59, is prominent in chapters 25 and 26 of the Acts of the Apostles. It was in addressing him that Paul felt compelled to appeal to Nero in Rome. And it was Festus who asked King Agrippa and Bernice to listen to Paul and help him formulate the accusation against the apostle.

Josephus, however, says little about him except that he subdued the robbers, murderers and imposters who were plaguing Jerusalem. He also records Festus' support for King Agrippa in his unsuccessful attempt to remove the wall which was blocking the view from his dining-room (*Antiquities 20:8:11*).

When Festus died after only two years in office, Nero appointed as his successor a man named Albinus in Alexandria. Thanks to Josephus we know that the delay in his arrival led to the death of James, the brother of Jesus, who had become such an important leader in the early Christian church in Jerusalem.

King Agrippa had just appointed a new high priest, Ananus, who was a Sadducee and thus prone to be 'very rigid in judging offenders'. Since for the moment there was no Roman Governor in the country, Ananus saw his opportunity. 'He assembled the Sanhedrin and brought before them the brother of Jesus who was called Christ, whose name was James, and some others. When he had formed an accusation against them as breakers of the law, he delivered them to be stoned' (*Antiquities 20:9:1*).

Many people, Josephus comments, disapproved of this and asked King Agrippa to convey their protest to

Ananus. Others went to meet Albinus as he came from Egypt, 'informing him that it was illegal for Ananus to assemble the Sanhedrin without his consent'. Albinus agreed with them and wrote angrily to Ananus 'threatening to punish him for what he had done', while King Agrippa 'deprived him of the high-priesthood when he had ruled only three months' (*Antiquities 20:9:1*).

The New Testament makes no mention of the death of James, but there is not the slightest reason for doubting what Josephus says. He was 24 years old at the time and would easily have recalled the whole episode.

The Roman Army
Long experience enabled Josephus to speak with confidence about the military might of the Romans.

'Anyone who will take a look at the organisation of their army in general will recognise that they hold their far-flung empire not as the gift of fortune but as the prize of valour. They do not wait for war to begin before handling their arms or take action only when some emergency arises, but as if born ready armed they never have a truce from training. Every man works as hard at his daily training as if he was already on active service. That is why they stand up so easily to the strain of battle. No indiscipline dislodges them from their regular formation, no panic incapacitates them, no toil wears them out, so victory over men not so trained follows as a matter of course.

'They never give the enemy a chance to catch them off their guard, for whenever they invade hostile territory they rigidly refuse battle until they have fortified their camp. If the ground is uneven it is thoroughly levelled, then a rectangular site is marked out and a perimeter wall constructed with a gate on each of the four sides. The camp is divided up by streets accurately planned: in the middle of the soldiers' huts are those for the officers, in the centre of which is the commander's headquarters, which resembles a shrine. It all seems like a mushroom town with market-place, workmen's quarters and orderly rooms. Thanks to the number and skill of the workers, the erection of the defences and the buildings inside is accomplished faster than thought. The men then go to their quarters unit by unit in a quiet and disciplined manner. Nothing whatever is done without orders. Private soldiers report by units to their centurions, the centurions to their superior officers.

'When camp is to be struck, the trumpet sounds and every man springs to his duty. Huts are instantly dismantled and all preparations made for departure. The trumpet sounds again and at once they load the mules and wagons and take their places like runners lined up and hardly able to wait for the starter's signal. For the third time the trumpets ring out and the announcer, standing beside the supreme commander, asks three times in their native language whether they are ready for war. Three times they enthusiastically shout "Ready", raising their right arms in martial fervour. And in battle too nothing is done on the spur of the moment or without plan. Careful thought precedes every action, so they meet with very few setbacks.

'Military exercises give the Roman soldiers not only tough bodies but determined spirits too. Training methods are partly based on fear, for military law demands the death penalty not only for leaving a post but even for trivial misdemeanours. The generals inspire more fear than the law, since by rewarding good soldiers they avoid seeming harsh towards the men they punish. In the field the whole army is a single body, so knit together are their ranks, so flexible their manoeuvres. When planning precedes action and the plans are followed by so effective an army, it is no wonder that in the east the Euphrates, in the west the ocean, in the south the plains of Africa, and in the north the Danube and the Rhine are the limits of their Empire. One might say with truth that the conquests are less remarkable than the conquerors' (*Wars 3:5:1-7*).

And the army did not only consist of Romans from Italy. Josephus often refers to soldiers who were Syrians or Arabs, 'serving in wars that were not the concern of their own nations' (*Wars 5:13:5*), to 'large contingents from royal allies' (*Wars 5:1:6*), and to 'so-called Macedonians, all just out of their teens, trained and equipped in the Macedonian manner' (*Wars 5:11:3*). He likes to name soldiers whose prowess would have been well-known to many of his original readers, such as Sabinus, 'whose skin was black' (*Wars 6:1:6*), Julian the reckless Bithynian (*Wars 6:1:8*), Rufus the tough and ingenious Egyptian (*Wars 7:6:4*), or Tiberius Alexander the Jew, so remarkably 'entrusted with the command of the armies, whom years of experience had made a most competent advisor amid the uncertainties of war' (*Wars 5:1:6*).

Discipline was extremely strict. 'The pickets stationed in front of every Roman camp are subject to a severe law that a man who quits his post under any pretext whatsoever must be executed' (*Wars 5:11:5*). To discourage carelessness, Titus executed a cavalryman whose horse had been stolen when he 'let it graze free and unbridled' while he was collecting firewood (*Wars 6:2:7*). In spite of this, 'each private was anxious to please his decurion, the decurion his centurion, the centurion his tribune, the tribunes their generals, while the generals rivalled each other for the Emperor's favour' (*Wars 5:12:2*).

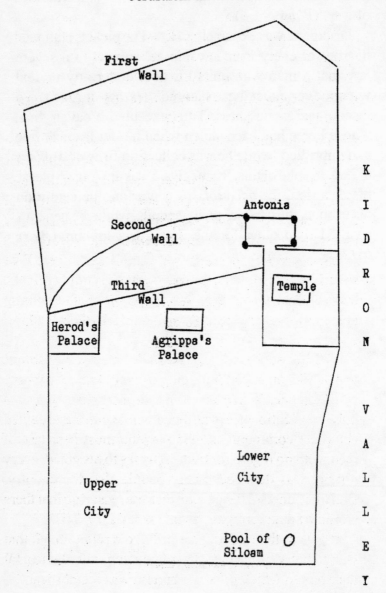

Jerusalem in 70 A.D.

5

The Siege and Destruction of Jerusalem

Josephus felt that Festus had been quite a good Governor (59-61), but his successor Albinus (62-64) acted very differently. Not content with crippling taxation and official measures which amounted to the looting of private property, he allowed men imprisoned for banditry to be bought out by their relatives. Only those who failed to pay were left in jail to serve their sentences. Free speech was completely suppressed and tyranny reigned everywhere. 'From then on, the seeds of the coming destruction were being sown in Jerusalem' (*Wars 2:14:1*).

Yet his successor, Gessius Florus, made Albinus appear like an angel. Indulging in every kind of robbery and violence, it was as though he had been sent as a public executioner. He stripped whole cities and ruined complete communities. 'He was the most heartless of men, with no regard for truth.' Thanks to his greed, every district was denuded. Many people fled the country. Daily he added to the general distress, ensuring that there would be a nation-wide revolt (*Wars 2:14:2-3*).

It was in the twelfth year of Nero's reign, in 66, that war actually broke out. 'In comparison with the fearful disasters to which it led, its pretext was insignificant' –

the endemic strife between Jews and Greeks in Caesarea, spilling over into Jerusalem, where 'Florus did what no one had ever dared to do, scourging and crucifying men who were indeed Jews but yet enjoyed Roman status' (*Wars 2:14:4-9*). Such atrocities provoked the Zealots to abandon all half measures. They achieved a remarkable success in capturing Masada by stealth and exterminating the Roman garrison, though it deluded them into thinking that with God on their side these aliens could be swept out of the land for good. Then, 'in spite of earnest appeals from the chief priests and prominent citizens, the Temple Captain, who was a very bold young man, persuaded the ministers of the Temple to abolish the sacrifices offered twice daily for Rome and the Emperor. It was this which made war with Rome inevitable' (*Wars 2:17:2, 2:10:4*). It seems remarkable that such sacrifices should ever have been offered, but Josephus maintains that it was consistent with Jewish law and piety. 'Moses, our legislator, nowhere forbids us to pay honours to worthy men, provided they are inferior to those we pay to God. Such honours testify to our respect for our Emperors and the Roman people. We offer no other such sacrifices. They are a special honour to the Emperors and to them alone' (*Apion 2:6*).

We have seen how the conflict erupted in Galilee, where Vespasian overwhelmed Josephus and his men at Jotapata. Similar disasters occurred all over the province. In gruesome detail Josephus describes the destruction of Magdala, the home of Mary Magdalene, and the large numbers who perished trying to escape across the Sea of

Galilee, 'the entire lake stained with blood and crammed with corpses' (*Wars 3:10:1-9*).

'When every place had been taken except the Herodium, Masada, and Machaerus, the target of the Romans was just Jerusalem itself' (*Wars 4:9:10*). But at that juncture Nero met his violent end, the three would-be Emperors were rapidly struck down, and Vespasian found that supreme power was likely to be his. His immediate reaction was to postpone the assault on Jerusalem, for he was anxious to get control of Alexandria, 'knowing that Egypt was the most important part of the Empire because it supplied corn' (*Wars 4:10:5*). So he and Titus went to Alexandria, taking Josephus with them, and it was there he was dramatically given his freedom, 'a man coming forward and severing the chain with one blow of an axe' (*Wars 4:10:7*). Vespasian then sailed for Rome, sending Titus with the pick of his army to destroy Jerusalem. Along with Josephus he went up the Nile (*Life 75*) and overland via Gaza and Joppa to Caesarea (*Wars 4:11:5*). Though no longer a prisoner, 'I was frequently in danger of being put to death, the Jews being very anxious to get me into their power and the Romans inclined to attribute any setback to my treachery' (*Life 75*).

Passover time was coming on. Only a few years earlier the Governor of Syria had ordered the chief priests to hold a census so that he could inform the Emperor of the number of his Jewish subjects. 'They chose to do this at the Passover Feast, at which sacrifice is offered from three to five in the afternoon. As it is not permissible to feast alone, a kind of fraternal group is formed around each victim, consisting of at least ten men, sometimes more. The count showed that there were 255,600 victims.' On this basis it was thought there were two and a half million people in Jerusalem as the tragedy unfolded (*Wars 6:9:3*).

Titus marched several of his legions inland from Caesarea, 'ordering the rest to meet him at Jerusalem'. Josephus was free to see with his own eyes the precise order in which the army advanced. Ahead went a guard of soldiers allied to the Romans, followed by roadmakers and camp constructors. Then came the officers' baggage under escort, preceding the mass of infantry, spearmen and cavalry surrounding Titus himself. Battering rams and other military engines were in the hands of a body of specially picked men commanded by tribunes and prefects, ahead of 'the Eagle surrounded by standards and trumpeters' just in front of the main body of the army, marching six abreast. At the very back came the baggage, servants, and 'mercenaries under the watchful eye of the rearguard' (*Wars 5:2:1*).

They passed through Samaria, spending one night at Gophna fifteen miles due north of the capital, and set off again at daybreak to 'pitch camp in the Valley of Thorns three and a half miles from Jerusalem'. Towards evening Titus went on with 600 cavalry to reconnoitre the city and see if the Jews could be 'frightened into surrender before a blow was struck'. There was no one to be seen, so he turned off the road with a handful of horsemen, riding 'over ground trenched for gardening, divided up by cross-walls and fences'. All of a sudden 'a horde of Jews poured out by the Women's Towers and cut them off.' Titus' escort grouped around him and succeeded in galloping through their assailants, but two men lost their lives, the first casualties in the siege which began that April day in 70 AD.

During the night the Fifth Legion arrived from Emmaus and at daybreak Titus ordered them and the Twelfth Legion to establish camps less than half a mile apart and only three-quarters of a mile from the city walls. He himself could see 'the shining mass of the Temple' from his headquarters on Mount Scopus. Then the Tenth Legion arrived from Jericho and began to build their camp on the Mount of Olives, 'which faces the city on the east and is separated from it by a deep ravine known as the Kidron' (*Wars 5:2:3*). Seeing three separate camps being constructed so close at hand, the Jews realised that 'war had indeed descended upon them in all its fury', but with the enemy scattered across the Mount they seized their opportunity, rushed out in force and inflicted considerable casualties before being forced back to the Kidron and up into the city again soon after midday (*Wars 5:2:4-5*).

After this experience Titus deployed a huge concentration of infantry, cavalry and archers close to the walls, equipped with quick-loading catapults and stone-throwers, to prevent further sorties. This enabled him to bring the army's baggage into the camps safely and to move his headquarters from Mount Scopus to a point only 400 yards from where the city wall bent back from north to west. Then he ordered the rest of his forces to level all the ground outside the city. 'Every fence and hedge which the occupiers had put round their gardens and orchards was thrown down, every fruit tree in the area felled, the dips and hollows filled in, the rocky projections demolished, and the whole space flattened from Mount Scopus to Herod's Monuments alongside the Serpents' Pool. This took four days.' Once it was done he employed the entire army collecting timber to build platforms (*Wars 5:3:2, 5:3:5*).

On its northern side Jerusalem was defended by three walls, 'Everywhere else it was surrounded by deep ravines and steep cliffs which made access impossible.' Titus' plan of action was to fight his way to each wall in turn, then hammer it day and night with his powerful battering rams till the legions could break through. For this the platforms were essential, raising the attackers to the level of the defenders or even higher, so that they could drive them off the walls and prevent them destroying the rams. The soldiers building the platforms 'were shielded from missiles by wicker screens laid across palisades'. Josephus describes the stone-throwing engines of the legions as masterpieces of construction. 'The stones weighed half a hundredweight and travelled over 400 yards. They were white, so not only were they heard whizzing through the air but their shining surface could easily be seen, so look-outs would give warning every time one came hurtling across, till the Romans took to blackening them. In spite of suffering many casualties, the Jews did not allow their enemies to raise the platforms in safety but fought valiantly day and night to stop them. Hundreds of firebrands were flung against the engines.' On the platforms the Romans erected towers, from which archers and lighter stone-throwers could pelt the defenders. On such lofty perches 'these men were beyond the reach of Jewish weapons and there was no way to capture the towers which were too heavy to overturn and were cased in iron so that they could not be set on fire'. Meanwhile engineers measured the distance from platform to wall by throwing lead and line, and when they found that battering rams could reach it they brought them up. Driven off the wall, the Jews were unable to prevent the biggest ram from gradually achieving its purpose. Once the wall was breached, the Romans climbed through, opened the gates, and let the whole army in, while the defenders ran back to the second wall. So after two weeks fighting, on May 7th, they demolished most of the first wall, along with the northern suburbs of the city (*Wars 5:6:2* to *5:7:1*).

It took only eight days for the legions to capture the second wall, though there was heavy fighting for a time, the Jews launching out courageously to grapple with them in hand-to-hand struggles. 'Neither side showed any sign of flagging. Assaults, wall-fightings and sorties at company strength went on continuously all day long. Dusk hardly availed to break off the battles begun at dawn. There was no sleep for either side, indeed the night was less endurable than the day, the Jews expecting every moment the capture of the wall, the Romans fearing an assault on their camps. Both passed the night in arms, yet the first glimmer of dawn found them ready for battle.' At last the defenders were compelled to withdraw as before and, once he was in possession of the wall, Titus destroyed it from end to end (*Wars 5:7:3* to *5:8:2*).

'The Romans then suspended the siege for a few days, hoping that the loss of the second wall and the fear of starvation would induce the Jews to surrender. When the soldiers' pay-day arrived, Titus ordered the officers to parade their men in full view of the Jews and there count over money to each man.' Decked out as finely as possible, infantry, cavalrymen and horses made a splendid sight. The whole length of the third wall and the north side of the Temple were packed with spectators, amazed at the magnificent display. But it did not have the desired effect, so Titus ordered the construction of four new platforms, two opposite the Upper City, two threatening the fortress of Antonia and the Temple (*Wars 5:9:1-2*).

At the same time, as he had often done before, Titus sent Josephus to talk to the defenders in their own language, thinking they would perhaps yield to the persuasions of a fellow-countryman. So he circled the wall, trying to keep out of range but within hearing, appealing to them again and again to spare their people, their country, and their Temple. 'I know that danger threatens my own mother and my wife,' he said, 'a famous family of great promise, and perhaps you think it is just for their sake that I am advising you.' Ignoring their howls of derision and showers of stones, he tried to explain to them at the top of his voice that 'God, who hands over dominion from nation to nation, now abides in Italy', reminding them that their ancestors had wisely submitted to Rome, which they would never have done had they not been convinced that 'God was on the Roman side' (*Wars 5:9:3*).

By this time famine had become as great a menace to the Jews as the Roman army surrounding them. 'All human feelings, alas, yield to hunger. When hunger reigns, restraint is abandoned' (*Wars 5:10:3*). Murder, torture and cannibalism became common in the doomed city. 'Men crawled out in the night as far as the enemy guardposts, hoping to collect wild plants and herbs.' Those who managed to get as far as neighbouring valleys in their desperate search for food were rounded up every day by cavalry and crucified in large numbers in full view of those manning the wall. 'In their rage and bitterness the soldiers nailed up their victims in various attitudes as a grim joke, till owing to the vast number there was no room for the crosses and no crosses for the bodies' (*Wars 5:11:1*). Titus cut off the hands of many other prisoners and sent them back into the city in that state as a warning to the population (*Wars 5:11:2*). In Josephus' opinion, 'we may sum it up by saying that no other city has ever endured such horrors' (*Wars 5:10:5*).

After seventeen days' continuous toil the four huge new platforms were ready for action and it seemed that the final assault was about to begin. However, with extraordinary ingenuity and determination the Jews had been tunnelling through the ground underneath the platforms opposite Antonia, which were close together.

The subterranean galleries they had created were supported with wooden props and packed with faggots daubed with pitch and bitumen, which were then ignited. 'As soon as the props were burnt away, the entire tunnel collapsed and with a thunderous crash the platforms fell into the cavity. At once there arose a dense cloud of smoke and dust as the flames were choked by the debris. This sudden blow filled the Romans with consternation' (*Wars 5:11:4*). On the other two platforms, some distance away, stone-throwers and batterers had already been assembled when both were entirely destroyed by a heroic band of Jews who succeeded in setting them on fire (*Wars 5:11:6*).

'Titus then held a council of war.' It was decided to build a wall right round the city to cut off all possibility of escape. 'Though it might well have taken months, the task was completed in three days.' The wall went 'through the Kidron, enclosing the Mount of Olives and the next eminence which overhangs the valley near Siloam'. Thirteen forts were made in the wall, which was patrolled every night (*Wars 5:12:1-2*).

To attack Antonia four more platforms had to be constructed, an arduous task because the whole area round the town to a distance of ten miles had already been stripped of trees. Having to go so far to find timber, the job took the Romans three weeks. 'The countryside was a pitiful sight. Where once had been lovely vistas of woods and parks there was now nothing but desert and tree stumps. No one who had seen the Old Judea and the glorious suburbs of the city and then set eyes on her present desolation could have helped groaning at so terrible a transformation. Every trace of beauty had been blotted out by the war' (*Wars 6:1:1*).

Meanwhile Josephus was sent to make another appeal for surrender but this time someone on the wall managed to hit him with a stone. The Jews ran out in hope of dragging him into the city, but Roman soldiers reached him first. 'They picked him up, though he knew little of what was going on. In Jerusalem it was thought he had been killed. No one was allowed to talk to his father, who was kept under lock and key, but when his mother was told in prison she said to the guards that she had foreseen this long ago and regretted that she would not be able to bury him.' However, he soon recovered and went on shouting to the men on the wall, many of whom were personally known to him (*Wars 5:13:2-3*).

It was after this incident that Arab and Syrian units in the Roman army, realising that Jewish deserters had often swallowed gold coins before escaping from the city, started ripping up any they could get hold of. Titus denounced such atrocities but, as Josephus observed, 'Avarice scorns every penalty, for an extraordinary love of gain is innate in man. So what the commander-in-chief forbade with threats was still done in secret, the foreign soldiers looking round first in case any Roman was watching' (*Wars 5:13:5*).

At this point in the siege Roman morale was low. The soldiers were amazed at the courage of the Jews and worn out by the struggle to rebuild the platforms. But they again brought up the battering rams to hammer the northern wall of Antonia, while the Jews pelted them with arrows, lumps of rock, and firebrands. Some of the legionaries, working feverishly under a roof of shields, used crowbars to lever stones out of the foundations. Then one dark night the tunnel, thanks to which the earlier platforms had been demolished, suddenly collapsed, dragging down a section of the wall. Hand to hand fighting followed with terrible carnage on both sides, till the Romans prevailed and Antonia was in their hands (*Wars 6:1:1-7*).

Slowly but surely the siege was approaching its culmination as 'battle raged continuously between small raiding parties from both sides' (*Wars 6:2:9*). The exhausted defenders still had some surprising successes. A united attack on the Roman posts across the Mount of Olives an hour before sunset nearly came off. And a solitary Jew, 'an insignificant man of small stature', went into an open space and challenged any Roman to single combat. As no one responded he mocked the legionaries for their cowardice, so a cavalryman took him on, but it was the Jew who won (*Wars 6:2:10*). His colleagues then withdrew from the western colonnade on the edge of the Temple area, having stacked it underneath with dry wood. A mass of Romans quickly erected ladders and swarmed across the roof, which the Jews then set on fire from end to end. Hardly any of the attackers survived. In retaliation they set fire to the entire northern colonnade to the point where it joined the eastern colonnade overhanging the Kidron Valley (*Wars 6:3:2*). At the same time the battering rams were 'pounding the wall of the outer Temple but making little impression on stones so huge and so perfectly bonded'. Titus then ordered numbers of ladders to be set up against the colonnades. At first the Jews did not react, but as soon as the soldiers came climbing up they assailed them with success, 'whole ladders crowded with infantry were pushed sideways at the top and overturned' (*Wars 6:4:1*).

At this point Titus called together his six senior generals to decide what they should do about the actual Temple, the inner Sanctuary itself. Josephus reports the three possibilities they discussed. Some insisted it should be destroyed because 'there would be continual revolts so long as the Temple remained as a rallying-point for Jews all over the world'. Others argued that it should be spared 'if the Jews evacuated it and no armed man was allowed inside'. Titus himself inclined to the view that, even if it was used as a fortress, such a great work of art ought to be preserved as an ornament for the Roman Empire. The commander of the Fifth Legion and Tiberius Alexander, the Jewish chief of staff, agreed with him (*Wars 6:4:3-4*).

So next day, August 10th, they planned to launch a full-scale attack, surround the Sanctuary, and if possible preserve it intact. In practice, however, 'the soldiers were like men possessed; there was no holding them, nor was there any arguing with the fire.' Although Titus went forward to the front line, 'his shouts were unheeded amid the distractions of battle and bloodshed.' Little children and old men, civilians and priests, all alike were butchered, held in the iron embrace of war, whether they defended themselves or cried for mercy. The Temple Hill, enveloped in flames from top to bottom, appeared to be boiling up from its very roots. In the last surviving colonnade of the outer Temple thousands of citizens had found refuge, but not one escaped. 'Their destruction was due to a false prophet who had just declared to the people in the city that God commanded them to go up into the Temple for deliverance. In adversity human beings are easily persuaded. When the deceiver actually promises deliverance from misery, the sufferer becomes the willing slave of hope. And so it happened that the unhappy crowds were beguiled by cheats and false messengers of God' (*Wars 6:4:8* to *6:5:2*).

Next day the Romans overran the Lower City and burnt the whole place 'as far as Siloam' (*Wars 6:7:2*). Without platforms they were unable to master the Upper City because it was so much higher. It took eighteen days to erect them. Then they brought up their battering rams and, finding the end of the war much easier than the beginning, were soon victorious without further loss. 'Pouring into the streets sword in hand, they cut down everyone they met and ferreted out those who had taken refuge in the sewers. At dusk the slaughter ceased but in the night fire gained the mastery, so on September 8th the sun rose over Jerusalem in flames' (*Wars 6:8:4-5*).

When all resistance had ceased, Titus put to death every elderly or infirm prisoner. 'Men in their prime who might be useful were herded into the Temple area and shut up in the Court of the Women. He picked out the tallest and handsomest youngsters to be kept for the triumphal procession in Rome. Those over seventeen were either sent to hard labour in Egypt or perished in provincial amphitheatres by the sword or wild beasts. Starvation disposed of 11,000 prisoners while the huge crowds were being sorted out' (*Wars 6:9:2*).

Josephus estimates that well over a million people lost their lives during the siege. 'The majority were Jews by race but not citizens of Jerusalem, for they had come together from the whole country for the Feast of Unleavened Bread and found themselves caught up in the disaster. No destruction ever wrought by God or man approached the wholesale carnage of this war' (*Wars 6:9:3*).

When there was no danger, Titus told Josephus he could take anything he liked from the ruins of his country, so he asked for the release of his parents, his brother, and two hundred others he knew. He was also allowed to rescue 'the holy books'. And Titus permitted him to go once to the Temple. 'On my way back I saw many captives crucified, three of whom I recognised. With tears in my eyes I told Titus, who at once ordered them to be taken down and cared for. Two died under the physician's hands, but the third recovered' (*Life 75*). The whole city and Temple were then 'so completely levelled to the ground that no one visiting the spot would believe it had once been inhabited'. Only a stretch of wall on the western side was left as a protection to the garrison, the Tenth Legion (*Wars 6:10:1* and *7:1:1*).

A dais was erected in the middle of what had been Titus' campsite. He took his stand there, flanked by his staff, so that the whole army could hear him. 'He thanked them for their unfailing loyalty to him, praising them for their obedience and personal heroism in many dangerous situations.' Officers then read out the names of men who had performed outstanding exploits. Calling them forward, Titus put golden crowns on their heads, promoted each one in rank, and assigned to them silver, gold and clothing from the spoils. 'Having offered prayers on behalf of the whole army, he sacrificed a large number of bullocks herded round the altars, dividing them among the troops for three days of feasting.'

'The voyage to Italy being impossible now that the summer was over', Titus marched north and stayed for the winter at Caesarea Philippi, 'where many of the prisoners perished, thrown to wild beasts or forced to fight each other in full-scale battles.' The same thing took place when he moved to Beirut, 'a town in Phoenicia, a Roman colony' (*Wars 7:1:2* to *7:3:1*). On his way to Egypt he called again at Jerusalem, 'contrasting the grievous desolation that met his eyes with the splendour of the city that was and the mighty structures once so beautiful but now in ruins.' It was the last sight Josephus was to have of his birthplace. They went on to Alexandria and made arrangements for 700 prisoners to be taken to Rome. Then they themselves sailed, Josephus merely saying that 'the voyage went according to plan' (*Wars 7:5:2-3*).

A few days after they arrived a tremendous triumphal procession was held to celebrate the victory. Josephus saw exactly what happened. During the previous night the soldiers marched out under their commanders and centurions and formed up round the Temple of Isis, where Vespasian and Titus had slept. 'Out of the immense population of the City not one person stayed at home. Everyone came and found a place somewhere, though there was only standing-room and barely enough space was left for the procession itself to pass.' The two generals sat on ivory chairs and after enthusiastic acclamations Vespasian called for silence. 'A complete hush fell on all and the Emperor, rising from his seat and wrapping most of his head in his cloak, offered the customary prayers, Titus also doing the same. He then made a short speech, dismissed the soldiers, and sacrificed to the gods that stand on either side of the gate through which triumphal processions always pass.'

Josephus felt it was impossible for him to give a full account of all the magnificent spectacles, works of art, treasures, rarities of nature, and other priceless marvels of many different peoples brought together that day to show the greatness of the Roman Empire. 'In the procession were also images of the Roman gods of wonderful size and artistic merit, all sorts of animals picturesquely decked out, and even the host of captives wore beautiful garments.' Travelling stages four storeys high caused a sensation, while numerous tableaux portrayed successive episodes in the war and displayed captured commanders still in their filthy rags. The most prominent of all the spoils were those taken from the Temple in Jerusalem, a heavy golden table, 'the crimson curtains of the inner Sanctuary', and 'the Jewish Law', possibly those 'holy books' which Josephus had been allowed to rescue. A special feature was the golden lampstand, 'the central shaft fixed to a base from which slender branches extended, the end of each forged into a lamp, seven of them.'

The procession halted at the Temple of Jupiter Capitolinus till word came that Simon, the Zealot commander-in-chief, 'dragged along with a noose round his neck while his escort knocked him about', had been put to death in the Forum, 'the spot laid down by the law of Rome for the execution of those condemned to death for their misdeeds'. Then followed 'universal acclamation, sacrifices, the customary prayers, sumptuous banquets and triumphant victory celebrations all day long.' Vespasian decided to erect a splendid Temple of Peace to contain all the treasures he had collected. 'It was there he laid up the golden vessels from the Temple of the Jews, but their Law and the crimson curtains of the Inner Sanctuary he deposited in the Palace for safe keeping' (*Wars 7:5:3-6*).

Only Josephus has recorded this terrible story for us. No account of it by any Roman historian has survived. Plutarch ends his long series of biographies with the Emperors killed in 69 AD and never refers to the war with the Jews. Neither does the younger Pliny. Tacitus may have touched on the subject, but his *Annals of Imperial Rome* breaks off in 66 AD. The only Roman writer who contributes in any way to the matter is Suetonius. In his biographies of Vespasian and Titus he makes a few brief allusions to what happened, telling us that 'Titus went to command one of his father's legions in Judea', and that 'in the final assault on Jerusalem Titus' prowess inspired deep admiration in the troops' (*The Twelve Caesars 10* and *11*).

Yet there is another source to which we can turn for allusion to that assault. Luke 19:37-44 records that forty years earlier, as Jesus was going down the Mount of Olives on what proved to be his final visit to Jerusalem, he saw the city spread out before him and wept over it, saying, 'If you, even you, had only known on this day what would bring peace – but now it is hidden from your eyes. The days will come upon you when your enemies will build an embankment against you and encircle you and hem you in on every side. They will dash you to the ground, you and your children within your walls. They will not leave one stone upon another.'

Returning to the Mount of Olives shortly afterwards, he reiterated this warning. 'When you see Jerusalem surrounded by armies, you will know that its desolation is near.... There will be great distress in the land and wrath against this people. They will fall by the sword and will be taken as prisoners to all the nations. Jerusalem will be trampled on by the Gentiles' (Luke 21:20-24). Similar words are preserved in Matthew 24 and Mark 13, which include the memorable declaration that 'those will be days of distress unequalled from the beginning, when God created the world, until now – and never to be equalled again' (Mark 13:19; Matthew 24:21).

The contrast between these brief predictions of the great disaster and Josephus' appallingly detailed account of their fulfilment is immense, yet in saying that 'no destruction ever wrought by God or man approached the wholesale carnage of this war' (*Wars 6:9:3*) he unconsciously echoes what Jesus had prophesied.

The Capture of Machaerus and Masada

After Titus had left, it fell to other Roman generals to finish off the entire campaign by conquering the almost impregnable fortresses of Machaerus and Masada, respectively east and just west of the Dead Sea. First they tackled Machaerus, planning to fill in the ravine on one side, but every single day the Jews showed remarkable initiative in launching surprise attacks.

'There was one particularly enterprising young man named Eleazer who did a lot of damage to the Romans in these encounters, smoothing the way to the attack for those who dared to sally out with him and making retreat safe by being the last to withdraw. One day when the battle had been broken off and both sides had retired, confidently supposing that none of the enemy would start fighting again, he stayed outside the gates talking to the defenders on the wall, with no thought for anyone else. A soldier from the Roman camp, an Egyptian named Rufus, saw his chance and performed a breath-taking feat. He made a sudden rush, picked the man up, armour and all, and before the spectators on the wall could recover from their astonishment carried him off to the Roman camp. The commander ordered him to be stripped, taken where he would be most clearly seen by the watchers in the town, and flogged.'

'The Jews were terribly distressed by Eleazer's agony, for he came from a large and eminent family. Realising this, the Roman commander ordered a cross to be set up, as though he was about to crucify him. At this many people inside the fortress began to plead on his behalf, while Eleazer himself implored them not to allow him to suffer the most humiliating of deaths but to save their own lives by submitting to the power of Rome. His appeal proved irresistible. Contrary to their nature the defenders yielded to pity and hastily despatched a delegation to discuss the surrender of the fortress, on the understanding that their lives would be spared and that they might take Eleazer away with them. The Romans agreed and did not break their word' (*Wars 7:6:4*).

That left only Masada, which proved a much more difficult operation. It was held by the Zealots under the command of an influential man also called Eleazer, 'a descendant of Judas the Galilean'. Mobilising all available forces, the Romans garrisoned the whole area, built a wall right round the rock to make escape impossible, and brought in drinking water from a considerable distance, as there was no spring in the neighbourhood at all. Then, over a period of two or three years and in the face of fierce resistance, they constructed a huge ramp on the western side, gradually building it up to the summit. The last night came and Eleazer knew that at dawn the Romans would overwhelm them. 'He also had a clear picture of what they would do to men, women and children when they won the day.' So he assembled his comrades and suggested to them that mass suicide was preferable to capture. 'Long ago we resolved not to serve the Romans but God,' he said. 'Now the time has come and I think it is God who has given us the privilege of dying nobly as free men. Man's calamity is not death but life. Death gives freedom to our souls and lets them depart to their own pure home, the freedom of eternity. Let us leave this world as free men, along with our wives and children.'

An irresistible desire to do the deed seized them all. 'With streaming eyes they embraced and caressed their wives, and taking their children in their arms pressed upon them the last lingering kisses. In the end not a man failed to carry out his terrible resolve.' When the Romans stormed onto the summit they found only two women, five little children and 960 dead bodies.

'One of the survivors, who was related to Eleazer and superior to most women in intelligence and education, provided them with a lucid report of Eleazer's speech and a detailed account of the action which followed.' But if it had not been for Josephus we would not have known anything about this famous episode in Jewish history, in proof of which the ramp is still there (*Wars 7:8-9*).

6

Districts and Towns

Galilee, Perea, Samaria and Judea

John 4:3-4: 'Jesus left Judea and went back once more to Galilee. Now he had to go through Samaria.'

Matthew 19:1: 'Jesus left Galilee and went into the region of Judea beyond the Jordan', usually called Perea.

'Small as Galilee is and encircled by powerful foreign neighbours, it has invariably held out against enemy attack, for the Galileans are fighters from the cradle. Never has cowardice afflicted the men or a declining population the country. The whole area is excellent for crops or cattle and rich in forests of every kind, so that it invites even those least inclined to work on the land. Consequently every inch has been cultivated and not a corner goes to waste. It is thickly studded with towns and innumerable villages' (*Wars 3:3:1-2*).

'Perea, though much greater in extent, is mostly a stony desert, too wild to produce cultivated crops. In some parts, however, the soil is workable and in the plains grow trees of many kinds, specially olives, vines and palms. The country is watered by mountain torrents and perennial springs. Its southern limit is Moab and on the east it shares a frontier with Arabia' (*Wars 3:3:3*).

'Samaria lies between Galilee and Judea. In character it is exactly like Judea, made up of hills and plains with soil which amply repays cultivation. Both are well-wooded and prolific in fruit, for rain is generally ample. Lush grass is so plentiful that the milk-yield of their cows is exceptionally heavy. The final proof of their outstanding productivity is the swarming population of both countries. Judea stretches from the River Jordan to Joppa and the coastal strip. Right in the middle lies the City of Jerusalem, raised above the whole neighbourhood as the head above the body' (*Wars 3:3:4-5*).

'Having given orders that a hundred men should get ready to go to Jerusalem, I wrote to my friends in Samaria to make sure they could pass safely through, as it was absolutely necessary for those who wanted to go quickly to Jerusalem to travel via Samaria, since by that road the journey from Galilee took only three days' (*Life 52*).

In his long account of events in the first century AD, Josephus never mentions either Bethlehem or Nazareth.

The Lake of Galilee and Gennesareth

Matthew 14:34: 'When they had crossed over they landed at Gennesareth.'

Luke 5:1: 'Jesus was standing by the Lake of Gennesareth.'

Josephus says, 'The Lake is known locally as Gennesareth, taking its name from the region adjoining it' (*Wars 3:10:1 and 7*).

'The Lake measures 16 miles by 4½. Its water is most delicious, clearer than marsh water and quite pure, as on every side it ends in a sandy beach. When drawn out it is pleasantly warm, more agreeable than river or spring water, yet always colder than one would expect from a lake of that size. The species of fish that live in the lake differ from those found elsewhere. After passing the city of Julia the River Jordan goes straight through the middle of the lake. Alongside Lake Gennesareth is a stretch of country with the same name, wonderful in its beauty and characteristics. Thanks to the rich soil there is not a plant that does not flourish there. The air is so temperate that it suits the most diverse species. Walnuts flourish but so do palms, side by side with figs and olives. One might deem it nature's crowning achievement to force together natural enemies into one spot and to bring the seasons into healthy rivalry, each as it were laying claim to the region. Figs and grapes flourish for ten months on end, the rest ripening all the year round, for it is watered by a spring with great fertilising power, known locally as the Capernaum. The length of the region measured along the shore of the lake is 3½ miles, the width 2½' (*Wars 3:10:7-8*).

The Jordan Valley and the Dead Sea

Luke 10:30: 'Jesus said, A man was going down from Jerusalem to Jericho when he fell into the hands of robbers.'

'Jericho is situated in a plain above which rises a treeless mountain range of very great length, stretching northwards to the Scythopolis district and southwards to the region of Sodom and the far end of the Dead Sea. This ridge is bare, uneven all the way, and uninhabited because of its infertility. On the other side of the Jordan rises a parallel range and the country between the two is called the Great Plain, measuring 140 miles long by 14 miles wide. It is bisected by the Jordan and has two lakes in it, the Dead Sea and Lake Tiberias. They are opposite in character, the former salt and sterile, the latter sweet and prolific. In summer the plain is burnt up and the absolute drought makes the air unwholesome. It is entirely waterless except for the Jordan, which is why the palms on the river-bank bear heavier crops than those at a distance. Near Jericho, however, there is an abundant spring, admirable for irrigation, gushing out near the old city. Here the rarest and loveliest things are found in plenty. It would be hard to find another region in the wide world to compare with it, so large is the yield from the seed sown, so it would be no exaggeration to call the place divine. I think it is due to the warmth of the air and the fertilising power of the water. The warmth draws out the growing plants, making them spread, while the moisture encourages root-growth in them all and supplies strength for the summer, when the district is so burnt up that no one goes out if he can help it. The air is so mild that the inhabitants dress in linen when the rest of Judea is under snow. The country between Jerusalem and Jericho is a rocky desert. Between Jericho and the Jordan or the Dead Sea lies the land of Sodom, once so rich in crops and in the wealth of its cities, but now dust and ashes. To this extent the stories about the land of Sodom are confirmed by the evidence of our eyes' (*Wars 4:8:2-4*).

'When Vespasian came to examine the Dead Sea, he ordered some non-swimmers to be thrown into deep water with their hands tied behind them. They all came to the surface' (*Wars 4:8:4*).

Arabia

Galatians 1:15-17: 'When God was pleased to reveal his Son in me. . .I went into Arabia and later returned to Damascus.'

'Arabia is a country that borders upon Judea' (*Antiquities 14:1:4*).

From a high tower in Jerusalem, in which for a time Titus had his headquarters, it was possible to see the Mediterranean in the west and 'get a view of Arabia at sunrise' in the east (*Wars 5:4:3*).

Cyrene

Luke 23:26: 'They seized Simon from Cyrene, put the cross on him, and made him carry it behind Jesus.'

Acts 11:20: 'Men from Cyprus and Cyrene went to Antioch and began to speak to Greeks also, telling them the good news about the Lord Jesus.'

'There are four classes of men in Cyrene: citizens, farmers, strangers, and Jews. The Jews are already to be found in all the cities. It is hard to find a place in the habitable earth that has not admitted this tribe of men. Egypt and Cyrene maintain great bodies of these Jews and have grown up to greater prosperity with them' (*Antiquities 14:7:2*).

Alexandria

Acts 18:24: 'A Jew named Apollos, an Alexandrian, came to Ephesus.'

'Alexandria, a city 3½ miles long and over a mile wide, so wealthy and with such a large population' (*Wars 2:16:4*).

'Alexander the Great, finding the Jews very ready to help him against the Egyptians, rewarded their active support with permission to reside in Alexandria with the same rights as the Greeks. They retained this privilege under his successors, who in addition assigned them a quarter for their exclusive use, so that they could preserve their own way of life uncorrupted by needless contact with other races' (*Wars 2:18:7*).

'The Jews are powerful in Egypt. Many were attracted to go there by the fertility of the soil. They are allowed an ethnarch who governs them and cares for them as if he were the ruler of a free republic' (*Antiquities 12:1:1* and *14:7:2*).

Antioch

Acts 11:26: 'The disciples were first called Christians at Antioch.'

'Antioch, the capital of Syria, by virtue of its size and prosperity undoubtedly the third city of the Roman Empire', after Rome and Alexandria (*Wars 3:2:4*).

'Men of Jewish blood are diffused in great numbers all over the world, specially in Syria where the two nations are neighbours. The biggest Jewish colony was at Antioch owing to the size of the city and still more because its rulers had made it safe for them to settle there, giving them the same privileges as the Greeks. They grew in numbers, all the time attracting to their worship a great many Greeks, making them virtually members of their own community' (*Wars 7:3:3*).

Capernaum

Matthew 4:12-13: 'When Jesus heard that John had been put in prison, he returned to Galilee. Leaving Nazareth, he went and lived in Capernaum which was by the lake.'

'The horse on which I rode and upon whose back I fought, fell into a quagmire and threw me to the ground. I was carried into a village called Capernaum. My soldiers were afraid I had been hurt worse than I was' (*Life 72*).

Ptolemais

Acts 21:7: 'We continued our voyage from Tyre and landed at Ptolemais, where we greeted the brothers and stayed with them for a day.' This is the city now known as Acre.

'Ptolemais is a Galilean seaside town, built on the edge of the great plain and shut in by mountains. Seven miles to the east is the Galilean range, fifteen miles south is Carmel' (*Wars 2:10:2*).

'Herod sailed out of Italy to Ptolemais, got together no small army and marched through Galilee' (*Antiquities 14:15:1*).

'Vespasian spent some time at Ptolemais with Titus organising his forces and then sent them to attack Jotapata' (*Wars 3:6:1*).

Puteoli

Acts 28:13-14: 'Next day the south wind came up and on the following day we reached Puteoli. There we found some brothers who invited us to spend a week with them. And so we went to Rome.' Puteoli is now Pozzuoli, just west of Naples.

'At dawn we sighted a ship of Cyrene and by God's providence eighty of us were rescued. When I had thus escaped and was come to Puteoli, I became acquainted with a Jewish actor much beloved by Nero' (*Life 3*).

7

Jewish Religion

The Pharisees

'The Pharisees count as the leading Jewish sect. Their opinion is that what God wills is what happens, yet that men are free to act as they think fit, virtuously or viciously. They believe in the immortality of the soul and in rewards and punishments after death. They say that those who live virtuously will have power to live again, but those who have lived viciously will be detained in an everlasting prison. The mass of the population, persuaded of the truth of these doctrines, perform whatever the Pharisees prescribe about divine worship, prayers, and sacrifices. On account of their teaching and their good conduct the Pharisees are greatly respected. Unlike the Sadducees, they are friendly to each other and seek to promote concord with the general public' (*Antiquities 18:1:3, Wars 2:8:14*).

'They delivered to the people a great many observances which are not written in the law of Moses at all but derived from their ancestors. They were specially believed when they spoke severely against others, even though it was only due to envy' (*Antiquities 13:10:6* and *13:15:5*).

The Sadducees

'The Sadducees suppose that God is in no way concerned whether we do good or evil. It is entirely up to us. We can act as we please. Both are open to us and the choice is our own.'

'They adhere strictly to the Law of Moses, arguing that we should not observe what is merely derived from tradition, as the Pharisees do. However, the only people they succeed in persuading of this are the rich, whereas the Pharisees have the populace on their side. Though not many agree with them, those who do are often important.'

'They believe that the soul dies with the body. They totally deny the immortality of the soul, as well as any punishment or reward after death' (*Antiquities 18:1:4, Wars 2:8:14*).

The Essenes

The Essenes are not mentioned in the New Testament, but Josephus admired them so much that he described them in detail. 'Although they are excluded from the Temple courts and offer their sacrifices by themselves, their way of life is superior to that of other men. This is shown by their custom of having everything in common. There are about four thousand men who live in this way, without wives or servants. Living by themselves, they serve each other and devote all their working time to farming' (*Antiquities 18:1:5*).

He depicts this movement withdrawn from ordinary society as 'Jews professing a severer discipline and showing a devotion to God in a way all their own'. They washed in cold water at noon every day and then 'assembled in a building of their own, which no one outside their community is allowed to enter'. They would then sit down to eat in silence, 'as if in a holy temple', giving thanks to God before and after the meal. 'They had no one city, but large colonies everywhere and like children in the care of a stern tutor, they take no action without orders from their supervisors.'

No one wishing to join them was admitted to their communal life for three years and then only after promising to cooperate with the good, hate the wicked, and 'never reveal any of their secrets to outsiders'. They were so intensely sabbatarian that they would not even 'ease themselves' on the seventh day. They rejected swearing, so 'every word they speak is more binding than an oath'. They were 'wonderfully devoted to the works of ancient writers and some of them, after a lifelong study of sacred literature and various purifications, claimed to be able to foretell the future'.

Josephus particularly emphasises Essene convictions about the immortality of the soul, which they regarded as 'trapped in the prison of the body'. On life after death 'They teach the same doctrine as the Greeks, that for good souls there waits a home beyond the ocean but for bad souls a dark abyss of punishment. In this way they hope to encourage virtue and discourage vice' (*Wars 2:8:2-12*).

The Zealots

Acts 5:34-39 records the speech to the Sanhedrin made by Gamaliel the Pharisee in which he referred to 'Judas the Galilean, who appeared in the days of the census and led a band of people in revolt. He was killed and all his followers were scattered.'

Josephus also mentions this man. 'Judas the Galilean was a very clever Rabbi' (*Wars 2:17:8*). 'He was the author of the fourth sect of Jewish philosophy, the Zealots (*Antiquities 18:1:6*).

'Judas said that taxation by the Romans was no better than an introduction to slavery and he exhorted the nation to assert their liberty. He maintained that God would not help them unless they rallied together for their own advantage and set about great exploits. All sorts of misfortunes sprang from him and his followers, for the nation was infected with this doctrine to an incredible degree. It was this system of philosophy which laid the foundation for our future miseries, for people received what they said with great pleasure' (*Antiquities 18:1:1*).

'In other matters they agreed with the Pharisees, but they had this intense attachment to liberty, insisting that God alone should be their ruler and lord. It was their immovable resolution not to call any man lord. No fear of death, their own or that of their relatives, made any difference to them. The nation began to grow mad with this distemper' (*Antiquities 18:1:6*).

All four lists of the twelve apostles in the New Testament included 'Simon the Zealot'. In Matthew and Mark the Greek word used is 'the Cananean', a term which does not mean Canaanite but is derived from the Aramaic word for 'Zealot'.

The Law of Moses

John 1:17: 'The law was given through Moses; grace and truth came through Jesus Christ.'

Luke 24:27: 'Beginning with Moses and all the Prophets, he explained to them what was said in all the Scriptures concerning himself.'

Acts 28:23: 'From morning till evening Paul explained and declared to them the kingdom of God and tried to convince them about Jesus from the Law of Moses and from the Prophets.'

'Moses, our legislator, became an excellent general of an army, a most prudent counsellor, taking the greatest care of all. While he made them obedient to him, he did not use his authority for his own private advantage but showed the great degree of virtue that was in him. He was no imposter, no deceiver. When he had first persuaded himself that his actions and designs were agreeable to God's will, he thought it his duty to impress on every one that those who believe God is the inspector of their lives will not permit themselves any sin. This is the character of our legislator. He ordained our government to be what may be termed a theocracy, ascribing authority and power to God, the author of all the good things enjoyed in common by mankind and by each one in particular. He represented God as unbegotten and immutable through all eternity, superior to all mortal conceptions, known to us by his power but unknown to us in his essence. Moses made his actions agree to his laws and so firmly imprinted this faith in God upon posterity that it can never be removed. He did not make religion a part of virtue, he made virtues part of religion, so that all our actions and words have reference to God. He very carefully combined instruction with action. Beginning from earliest infancy he left nothing to be done at the pleasure of the person himself. He made a fixed rule of law, from what food they should abstain, what communion they should have with others, what diligence in their occupations, what times of rest, so that by living under that law as under a father and a master we might be guilty of no sin. So he permitted people to leave off their work and assemble to hear the law, not once or twice but every week, so that it is engraven on our souls. Where shall we find a better or more righteous constitution? What is there in it that anyone would want to change? What can be invented better? What more worthy worship can be paid to God than we pay?' (*Apion 2:17-23*).

The Courts of the Temple

Some English versions of the New Testament distinguish between the Temple area as a whole, with its extensive courtyards and colonnades, and the relatively small Sanctuary, to which only priests had access.

John 10:23: 'Jesus was in the temple area, walking in Solomon's Colonnade.'

Mark 11:15-16: 'Jesus entered the temple area and began driving out those who were buying and selling there. He would not allow anyone to carry anything through the temple courts.'

Luke 20:1: 'Jesus was teaching the people in the

temple courts and preaching the gospel.'

Acts 2:46: 'Every day the believers continued to meet together in the temple courts.'

Acts 5:21: 'At daybreak they entered the temple courts and began to teach the people.'

Acts 21:27-29: 'Some Jews from the province of Asia saw Paul at the temple. They stirred up the whole crowd and seized him, shouting, "He has brought Greeks into the temple area and defiled this holy place." '

'The eastern cloisters, which belonged to the outer court, were the work of King Solomon, who first of all built the entire Temple' (*Antiquities 20:9:7*).

'Herod encompassed the entire Temple with very large cloisters' (*Antiquities 15:11:3*).

'Our temple had four separate courts, encompassed by cloisters. Each of them had by our law a special degree of separation from the others. Everybody was allowed to go into the first court, even foreigners: none but women during their uncleanness were prohibited from passing through it. All Jews, as well as their wives when free from all uncleanness, could go into the second court. Jewish men, when they were clean and purified, might go into the third court. Only priests, wearing their sacerdotal garments, might go into the fourth court. None but the high priests, wearing their special robes, went into the most sacred place. It is not lawful to carry any vessel or anything relating to food or drink into the temple' (*Apion 2:8*).

'A few steps led up from the first court to the second, which was surrounded by a stone wall with an inscription on it forbidding any foreigners to go in on pain of death. On its eastern side was a large gate, through which such as were pure came in, together with their wives. The court beyond that was not allowed to the women. And still further in was another court not lawful for anyone to enter except the priests. The temple itself was inside that' (*Antiquities 15:11:5*).

'The colonnades of the first court were 45 feet wide and the complete circle of them measured three-quarters of a mile. They were supported by a double row of white marble pillars 37 feet high. Anyone passing through this towards the second court found it enclosed within a stone balustrade, in which slabs stood at regular intervals announcing the law of purification, some in Greek, some in Latin. No foreigner was to enter the Sacred Precincts, the name give to the second court, a rectangular area to which fourteen steps led up. Beyond these was a space from which flights of five steps led up to ten gates, two on the east side where a special place was walled off for the women to worship in. The Court of the Women could also be entered by one north gate and one south gate: women were not admitted through the other gates. Their court was open not only to native women but also to Jewesses from abroad. Nine of the ten gates were completely covered with gold and silver, but the one outside the Sanctuary was of even more valuable Corinthian bronze. Each gateway had double doors, each half being 45 feet high and 22 feet wide' (*Wars 5:5:2-3*).

Parallels to New Testament Passages

Living in the Desert

Matthew 3:1-4: 'In those days John the Baptist came preaching in the desert of Judea. John's clothes were made of camel's hair and he had a leather belt round his waist. His food was locusts and wild honey.'

'When I was informed that a man named Banus lived in the desert, used no clothing except what grew on trees, had no other food than what grew of its own accord, and bathed himself in cold water frequently night and day to preserve his chastity, I imitated him and continued with him for three years' (*Life 2*).

In a Dream

Matthew 27:19: 'While Pilate was sitting on the judge's seat, his wife sent him this message, "Don't have anything to do with that innocent man, because I have suffered a great deal today in a dream on account of him."'

'Before Archelaus was summoned to Rome by Augustus he saw in a dream nine full ears of corn devoured by oxen. An Essene suggested to him that each ear of corn meant a year when he would rule. Five days after hearing this he was called to his trial' (*Wars 2:7:3*).

'I think I might also mention the dream of his wife

Glaphyra. She had first married Alexander, brother of Archelaus, whom their father Herod put to death, then the King of Libya. When he died, Archelaus fell so deeply in love with her that he divorced his wife and married her. One night in a dream she saw Alexander standing by her, at which she rejoiced, embracing him with great affection. But he upbraided her, "O Glaphyra, didn't you pledge your faith to me? Weren't you married to me when you were a virgin? Didn't we have children together? Have you forgotten the love I bore you? But I won't forget it. I will set you free and you shall be mine again, as once you were." Two days later she died. There is something to be learnt from this. It confirms belief in the immortality of the soul and in God's providence over human affairs. If anyone does not believe such things, let him enjoy his own opinion without hindering another who would thereby encourage himself in virtue' (*Wars 2:7:4.* with *Antiquities 17:13:4-5*).

Corban

Mark 7:11: 'Whatever help you might otherwise have received from me is Corban, that is, a gift devoted to God.'

'The oath called Corban can only be found among the Jews. It declares what may be called "a thing devoted to God"' (*Apion 1:22*).

'Pilate stirred up further trouble by expending the sacred treasure known as Corban on an aqueduct fifty miles long. This roused the population to fury' (*Wars 2:9:4*).

A Cup of Water

Mark 9:41: 'Anyone who gives you a cup of water because you belong to Christ will certainly not lose his reward.'

'Herod Agrippa was led about bound, even in his purple garments. It was extremely hot weather, so he was very thirsty. He saw a slave, whose name was Thaumastus, carrying water in a jug, so he asked if he could have a drink. The slave consented. He drank heartily and said, "If I once get clear of my bonds, I will reward you for this and get you your freedom." He kept his word, for when he came to the kingdom he took particular care of Thaumastus, secured him his liberty and made him his steward. The man grew old in that honourable task' (*Antiquities 18:6:6*).

The Sanhedrin

Mark 14:55: 'The chief priests and the whole Sanhedrin were looking for evidence against Jesus so that they could put him to death.'

Acts 6:12: 'They seized Stephen and brought him before the Sanhedrin.'

Acts 23:1: 'Paul looked straight at the Sanhedrin and said, "I have fulfilled my duty to God in all good conscience to this day." '

'As soon as I was come into Galilee and had learned the state of things, I wrote to the Sanhedrin at Jerusalem and asked what I should do' (*Life 12*).

'Our law has forbidden us to kill any man, however wicked, unless he has first been condemned to suffer death by the Sanhedrin' (*Antiquities 14:9:3*).

Quirinius

Luke 2:2: 'This was the first census that took place while Quirinius was governor of Syria.'

'Quirinius was sent as censor into Judea' (*Wars 7:8:1*).

'Quirinius, a Roman senator who had been consul and who on other accounts was of great dignity, was sent by Caesar into Syria. He came to Judea, which was part of Syria, to take account of its economy and to dispose of Archelaus' money' (*Antiquities 18:1:1*).

Annas, the high priest

Luke 3:2: 'During the high priesthood of Annas and Caiaphas the word of God came to John.'

John 18:13: 'They bound Jesus and brought him first to Annas.'

'This Annas proved a most fortunate man, for he had five sons who all held the office of high priest to God after he had himself held that dignity for a long time. This has never happened to any other of our high priests' (*Antiquities 20:9:1*).

Lysanias, tetrarch of Abilene

Luke 3:1-2: 'In the fifteenth year of the reign of Tiberius Caesar, when Pontius Pilate was governor of Judea, Herod tetrarch of Galilee, his brother Philip tetrarch of Iturea and Trachonitis, and Lysanias tetrarch of Abilene. . . .the word of God came to John.'

Neither the districts of Iturea, Trachonitis or Abilene – all north of the Lake of Galilee – nor the name of Lysanias are mentioned again in the New Testament, but each occurs several times in the writings of Josephus.

Abilene was near Damascus. Lysanias seems to have been a hereditary name borne by different people.

'Gaius gave Herod Agrippa the tetrarchy of Lysanias' (*Antiquities 18:6:1*).

'Abila of Lysanias and all that lay at Mount Lebanon were bestowed on Herod Agrippa by Claudius' (*Antiquities 19:5:1*).

After Herod Agrippa's death, this was confirmed to his son.

'Claudius gave King Agrippa Trachonitis with Abila, which last had been the tetrarchy of Lysanias' (*Antiquities 20:7:1*).

Josephus also alludes to 'the kingdom of Lysanias', 'the estate of Lysanias', and 'the house of Lysanias'.

Advice to Soldiers

Luke 3:14: 'Then some soldiers asked John, "And what should we do?" John replied, "Don't extort money and don't accuse people falsely: be content with your pay." '

'I advised the soldiers not to fight with anybody nor to spoil the country, but to be content with what they had brought with them' (*Life 47*).

The Samaritans

John 4:9: 'You are a Jew and I am a Samaritan woman. How can you ask me for a drink? For Jews do not associate with Samaritans.'

John 4:20: 'Our fathers worshipped on this mountain, but you Jews claim that the place where we must worship is in Jerusalem.'

Luke 9:52: 'They went into a Samaritan village to

get things ready for him, but the people there did not welcome him because he was heading for Jerusalem.'

'When the Samaritans see the Jews in prosperity, they pretend that they are their kinsmen, descended from Joseph. But when they see the Jews in adversity they deny that they are in any way related to them, which is true' (*Antiquities 9:14:3* and *11:8:6*).

'The Jews said that according to the law of Moses the Temple was to be built at Jerusalem, but the Samaritans said it was to be built at Mount Gerizim, which they look upon as the holiest of all mountains' (*Antiquities 13:3:4* and *18:4:1*).

'It was the custom of the Galileans, when they came to the holy city at the festivals, to travel through the country of the Samaritans. At this time there lay in the road they took a village where the people fought them and killed many of them' (*Antiquities 20:6:1*).

The Pool of Siloam
John 9:7: 'Jesus said to him, "Go, wash in the pool of Siloam." So the man went and washed and came home seeing.'

'Siloam, the name we give to that sweet, never failing spring, the fountain of Siloam' (*Wars 5:4:1*).

Matthias
Acts 1:23-26: 'They proposed two men, Joseph and Matthias. Then they prayed, "Lord, you know everyone's heart. Show us which of these two you have chosen." Then they drew lots, and the lot fell to Matthias, so he was added to the eleven apostles.'

'My father Matthias was well-known in Jerusalem, the greatest city we have. I was brought up with my brother, whose name was Matthias' (*Life 1-2*). His grandfather's name was Joseph, but his great-grandfather and great-great-grandfather were both called Matthias. This suggests the name was quite common at that time.

Foreigners worshipping at Jerusalem

Acts 8:27-28: 'An Ethiopian eunuch, an important official in charge of all the treasury of Candace, Queen of the Ethiopians, had gone to Jerusalem to worship and on his way home was sitting in his chariot reading the book of Isaiah the prophet.'

'Helena, Queen of Adiabene, and her son Isates changed their course of life and embraced the Jewish customs. She had a mind to go to Jerusalem in order to worship at that Temple of God which was so famous among all men, her son conducting her a long way on her journey' (*Antiquities 20:2:1* and *5*).

'I am so bold as to say that we have become the teachers of other men. The multitude of mankind has for a long time had a great inclination to follow our religious observances' (*Apion 2:40* and *42*).

'Foreigners, who came from abroad in large numbers to be present at the Passover ceremonies, were not permitted to partake of the sacrifice' (*Wars 6:9:3*).

Watching the Gates

Acts 9:24: 'Day and night they kept close watch on the city gates in order to kill him.'

'I thought out a stratagem and at once placed those of my friends on whom I could rely at the gates to watch very carefully who went out at those gates' (*Life 32*).

The gate opening by itself

Acts 12:10: 'They passed the first and second guards and came to the iron gate leading to the city. It opened for them by itself and they went through it.'

'One of God's warnings which foreshadowed the coming desolation was that at midnight the East Gate of the Inner Sanctuary, made of bronze and so massive that it required twenty men to shut it every evening, opened by itself' (*Wars 6:5:3*).

Jews expelled from Rome

Acts 18:1-2: 'At Corinth Paul met a Jew named Aquila who had recently come from Italy with his wife Priscilla, because Claudius had ordered all the Jews to leave Rome.'

'Four wicked Jews living in Rome persuaded a woman of great dignity who had embraced the Jewish religion to send valuables to the Temple at Jerusalem. When they got them they spent all the money themselves. Her husband told the Emperor Tiberius who, after making enquiries, ordered all Jews to be banished from Rome' (*Antiquities 18:3:5*).

Tents

Acts 18:2-3: 'Paul went to see them and, because he was a tent-maker as they were, he stayed and worked with them.'

When the Roman President of Syria met the King of Parthia on a bridge over the Euphrates, 'Herod the Tetrarch erected a fine tent in the middle and made them a feast there' (*Antiquities 18:4:5*).

A Vow and a Haircut

Acts 18:18: 'Paul had his hair cut off at Cenchrea because of a vow he had taken.'

'Bernice was staying in Jerusalem to perform a vow to God. It is usual for those who are sick or in distress to vow that for thirty days before they intend to sacrifice they will abstain from wine and shave their heads. These vows Bernice was then performing' (*Wars 2:15:1*).

The Beach at Tyre

Acts 21:3-5: 'We landed at Tyre. Finding disciples there, we stayed seven days with them. When we left, all the disciples, with their wives and children, accompanied us out of the city and we knelt down on the shore and prayed.'

'A thousand Jews came to Tyre to meet Antony. Herod went out to them, for they were standing on the shore outside the city' (*Antiquities 14:13:2*).

When they were silent

Acts 21:40–22:1: 'Paul stood on the steps and motioned to the crowd. When they were all silent, he said to them in Aramaic, "Brothers and fathers, listen now to my defence." '

'I committed the care of my life to God and made haste to go out to the crowd. When they were silent I said to them, "My countrymen, I want to tell you the truth of this matter" ' (*Life 28-29*).

Ananias, the high priest

Acts 23:2: 'Ananias ordered those standing near Paul to strike him on the mouth.'

Acts 24:1: 'Ananias went down to Caesarea with some of the elders and a lawyer named Tertullus, and they brought their charges against Paul before Felix the governor.'

'They rushed in and burnt down the house of Ananias the high priest. He and other leading citizens fled to the palace and lost no time in bolting the doors. Next day Ananias was caught hiding near the palace canal. They murdered him' (*Wars 2:17:6* and *9*).

Kind treatment

Acts 24:23: 'Felix ordered the centurion to keep Paul under guard but to give him some freedom and allow his friends to take care of his needs.'

'The centurion and soldiers guarding Herod Agrippa were gentle and kindly, so he was allowed to bathe every day and his friends came to care for him, bringing him food' (*Antiquities 18:6:7*).

The Fast

Acts 27:9: 'Much time had been lost and sailing had already become dangerous, because by now it was after the Fast.'

'As winter was coming on, he thought it not safe to go to sea later' (*Antiquities 16:2:1*).

When Pompey captured Jerusalem in 63 BC, 'the city was taken on the day of the Fast' (*Antiquities 14:4:3*).

Exactly 27 years later Herod first took Jerusalem 'on the solemnity of the Fast' (*Antiquities 14:16:4*).

Throwing cargo overboard
Acts 27:18: 'We took such a violent battering from the storm that the next day they began to throw the cargo overboard.'

'Herod was hurrying to Rome even though the weather was stormy, so he set sail from Alexandria, but falling into a violent storm he had great difficulty in escaping to Rhodes with the loss of the ship's cargo' (*Antiquities 14:14:2-3*).

Giving the Right Hand
Galatians 2:9: 'James, Peter, and John gave me and Barnabas the right hand of fellowship. They agreed that we should go to the Gentiles and they to the Jews.'

'The people of the town had given their right hand and made a league with the President of Syria' (*Life 8*).

'Augustus came into Syria after Herod had reigned for seventeen years and the people were clamouring against his tyranny, but Caesar gave him his right hand and continued to treat him kindly' (*Antiquities 15:10:3*).

Heavily Armed
Ephesians 6:13: 'Put on the full armour of God, so that when the day of evil comes, you may be able to stand your ground, and after you have done everything, to stand.'

'Roman soldiers are armed with breastplate and helmet, a sword on each side, an axe and a pick, a basket, a strap, a saw, a bill-hook, a chain, and three days rations, so that an infantryman is almost as heavily laden as a pack-mule' (*Wars 3:5:5*).

The Praetorian Guard

Philippians 1:13: 'It has become known throughout the whole praetorian guard and to all the rest that my imprisonment is for Christ.'

'The whole palace was full of the soldiers' madness and even the Emperor's guards seemed under the same fear as the general population. The band called praetorian, which was the purest part of the army, was in consultation what to do at this juncture, how best to take care of themselves' (*Antiquities 19:3:1*).

The Scythians

Colossians 3:11: 'Here there is no Greek or Jew, circumcised or uncircumcised, barbarian, Scythian, slave or free, but Christ is all and is in all.'

'The Scythians differ little from brute beasts and take pleasure in killing' (*Apion 2:38*).

'A very large Scythian tribe crossed to the right bank of the Danube, overran the whole province and stripped it bare' (*Wars 7:4:3*).

'A Scythian tribe living near the River Don and the Sea of Azov, made a prolonged raid into Armenia, turning the countryside into a desert, carrying off most of the population and vast booty' (*Wars 7:7:4*).

The town of Bethshan, to the walls of which the bodies

of Saul and his sons were fastened, 'is called Scythopolis by the Greeks' (*Antiquities 12:8:5*).

'Scythopolis, not far from Tiberias, is the biggest city of the Decapolis' (*Wars 3:9:7*).

The Daily Sacrifice
Hebrews 7:26-27: 'Such a high priest meets our need – one who is holy, blameless, pure, set apart from sinners, exalted above the heavens. Unlike the other high priests, he does not need to offer sacrifices day after day, first for his own sins and then for the sins of the people. He sacrificed for their sins once for all when he offered himself.'

'They offered sacrifices and what were called the daily sacrifices and the oblations proper for the Sabbaths and all the festivals' (*Antiquities 11:4:1*).

'The constant practice of offering a daily sacrifice' (*Wars 1:1:1*).

'The sacrifice called "The Daily Sacrifice" ' (*Wars 6:2:1*).

'Anyone may learn what great piety we exercise towards God and the observance of his laws from the fact that fear did not hinder the priests from carrying out their sacred ministrations during the siege, for twice each day, in the morning and at about the ninth hour, they still offered their sacrifices on the altar' (*Antiquities 14:4:3*).

The Curtain of the Temple
Hebrews 9:1-3: 'Now the first covenant had regulations for worship and also an earthly sanctuary. A tabernacle

was set up. In its first room were the lampstand, the table, and the consecrated bread; this was called the Holy Place. Behind the second curtain was a room called the Most Holy Place.'

'The Sanctuary itself, the Holy Temple, was reached by a flight of twelve steps. It was two storeys high and was divided into two chambers. The gate was covered all over with gold. Passing through the gate one entered the ground-floor chamber, 90 feet high, 90 feet long, and 30 feet wide. The length was divided. In the first part, partitioned off at 60 feet, were three most wonderful world-famous works of art, a lampstand with seven branching lamps, a table, and an altar of incense. The inmost chamber was 30 feet long and was separated by a curtain from the outer part. Nothing at all was kept in it. It was unapproachable, inviolable, and invisible. It was called the Holy of Holies' (*Wars 5:5:4-5*).

'The high priest put on more ornate garments when he entered the Holy of Holies, which he did once a year, alone' (*Wars 5:5:7*).

Matthew 27:50-51: 'When Jesus had cried out again in a loud voice, he gave up his spirit. At that moment the curtain of the Temple was torn in two from top to bottom.'

Hebrews 10:19: 'We have confidence to enter the Most Holy Place by the blood of Jesus, by a new and living way through the curtain.'

Epilogue

The Kingdom of Iron and
the Kingdom of God

During the final decade of the first century Josephus was busy composing *The Antiquities of the Jews* for the enlightenment of his Roman contemporaries.

Sixty years had gone by since Jews had first been challenged by the words of Jesus and almost forty years since Paul wrote his Epistle to the Christians in Rome. The final paragraphs of the Acts of the Apostles tell us that only three days after Paul reached the capital himself, he called together the leaders of the Jews, making it clear that he would like to address them. They were pleased. 'We want to hear what your views are, for we know that people everywhere are talking against this sect.' So they made an appointment and came in large numbers to where he was staying. 'From morning till evening he explained and declared to them the kingdom of God and tried to convince them about Jesus from the Law of Moses and from the Prophets. Some were convinced by what he said, but others would not believe' (Acts 28:17-24). After that, for the next two years he remained there, preaching and teaching boldly about the Lord Jesus Christ (Acts 28:30-31). Then Christians were in the public eye in a very different way when Nero killed many of them whom he chose to blame for the fire which ravaged Rome in 64 AD. So in the second half of the first century any intelligent Jew living in Rome, such as Josephus, would have had some idea of what Christianity was all about.

In the course of his long historical survey Josephus came to relate how the prophet Daniel interpreted to Nebuchadnezzar, King of Babylon, the dream he had had about an enormous image made of gold, silver, bronze and iron, which was smashed to pieces by 'a stone cut out but not by human hands', which replaced it, becoming a huge mountain, filling the whole earth (Daniel 2:31-35). Daniel explained that the gold, the silver and the bronze symbolised kingdoms which would be succeeded by a fourth 'strong as iron', but that then 'the God of heaven will set up a kingdom that shall never be destroyed'. He boldly told Nebuchadnezzar that 'it will crush all those kingdoms and bring them to an end, but it will itself endure for ever' (Daniel 2:36-45).

In his book Josephus points out how true it was that the Roman Empire, 'the kingdom of iron', had succeeded the Babylonians, the Perisans and the Greeks. But what was he to put down about the kingdom of God, which Daniel said would supplant it? How could he, totally dependent on the goodwill of the Roman Emperor, deal with that?

Whatever his own opinion may have been, he decided to err on the side of caution. 'Daniel told the King the meaning of the stone,' he wrote (*Antiquities 10:10:4*), 'but I do not think it proper to relate it, since I have only undertaken to describe things present or past, not things future. But if anyone is very eager to know what is true, reluctant to curb his curiosity, wanting to understand the uncertainties of the future, let him be diligent in reading the book of Daniel, which he will find among the sacred writings.' Under the circumstances Josephus falls short of explaining what was meant by the stone, that 'living stone, rejected by men but chosen by God' (1 Peter 2:4-8; Mark 12:10), yet one might feel that Jesus could have addressed to him what he said to another Jew who spoke wisely, 'You are not far from the kingdom of God' (Mark 12:34).

Subject index

*Pages in bold type indicate principal references

Scripture Index